"A brilliantly original ... twenty-first century. ... recommend this book ... to preserve it."

"This book is a profoundly positive, direct, and practical manual for bringing the human soul into harmony with the ways of the Earth."

"Movingly personal, a new formula for environmental enlightenment. A work of passion and clarity. Let us hope every nature lover in the nation will read it."

"This book changed the way I think and it will do the same for you. Destined to be a truly important book."

A Field Guide
to the Soul

A Down-to-Earth Handbook
of Spiritual Practice

James Thornton

BELL TOWER
New York

Grateful acknowledgment is made to the following for permission to reprint
previously published material:

Excerpts from *The Epic of Gilgamesh*, translated by N. K. Sandars (Penguin
Classics 1960, Second revised edition 1972). Copyright © 1960, 1964, and
1972 by N. K. Sandars. Reproduced by permission of Penguin Books Ltd.

Excerpts from *Dante's Inferno*, a new verse translation by Peter Thornton.
Copyright © 1998 by Peter Thornton. Reprinted by permission of the author.

Published by Bell Tower, an imprint of Harmony Books,
New York, New York
Member of the Crown Publishing Group.

Originally published in hardcover by Bell Tower in 1999.
First paperback edition published in 2000.

Random House, Inc. New York, Toronto, London, Sydney, Auckland
www.randomhouse.com

Bell Tower and colophon are registered trademarks of Random House, Inc.

Printed in the United States of America

Design by Jennifer Ann Daddio

Library of Congress Cataloging-in-Publication Data

Thornton, James, 1954–
A field guide to the soul : a down-to-earth handbook of spiritual
practice / James Thornton.
1. Spiritual life. 2. Nature—Religious aspects. I. Title.
BL624.T465   1999
291.4'4—dc21   98-24919
CIP

ISBN 0-609-80392-1

10   9   8   7   6   5   4   3   2

To Catherine and Peter Thornton, my parents,

and Alice Rogan, my aunt,

whose love runs deep and true and never fails,

&

Bill Melton and Patricia Smith,

whose belief and support made this book possible

Contents

4. THE WAY OF THE MIND

5. THE WAY OF THE HEART

6. THE WAY OF ACTION

Contents

Acknowledgments

To Martin Goodman, my partner in life, who led me into the way of the heart, gave me the courage to write, shared inspirations over a thousand cups of morning tea, read and edited two versions of this book, contributed endlessly to it, kept me reasonably sane while writing it, stayed patient through all of it, and keeps opening the door of love daily, my unending thanks.

My thanks to Bill Melton and Patricia Smith for their generous support, and equally generous belief in the value of the work, without which this book would never have been written, and to Charlie Halpern, president of the Nathan Cummings Foundation, who helped found Positive Futures, making an inquiry into our spiritual relationship with the Earth my daily work and practice.

My thanks to friends who read my manuscript and offered valuable advice. First to my father, Peter Thornton, who gave me the full benefit of a lifetime's accumulated legal acumen and human wisdom in two exhaustive readings, and whose blessing means the world. To Richmond Mayo-Smith for his skillful enthusiasm and a generosity that saw the next project started before this one was finished. To my brother, Peter Thornton, for his felicitous Dante and his fine example. And to Jonathan Kaufelt, Mark Matousek, Colleen Kelly, Barbara

Graham, Theodore Roszak, Peter Matthiessen, Ralph Metzner, James Broughton, Robert Weisz, and John Adams, all of whose advice and encouragement helped shape this book for the better.

Thanks to Toinette Lippe, my editor, whose extraordinary work with the text made it feel as though I had found a master botanist for the gardens of my mind, and whose belief in my message is why this book has come to see the light of day, and to Andrew Blauner, my agent, for his unfailing courtesy and unflagging belief in me.

Thanks to Christobel Haward, for providing an inspiring home in the French Pyrenees, where much of this book was written, and to Marion and Allan Hunt-Badiner, whose house in Big Sur provided sanctuary for writing an early draft.

Thanks to Flloyd Kennedy and Tamar Kotoske, who patiently typed various versions of the manuscript and offered valuable editorial suggestions.

Thanks, too, to a host of friends who offered help and insight along the way, including Robbie Lamming, Susan Goodman, Mike Finney, Rand Lee, Philippa Calnan, Gary Reichelderfer. And to Deirdre Mullane, for first seeing the value in this project.

And finally thanks to the Earth herself, our loving, boundless Mother.

1

Invitation
to a Journey

A Beginning

An ancient Chinese curse runs like this: "May you live in interesting times." We certainly live in interesting times. And yet we can transform our troubles into strength and our darkness into awakening when we know how. We can know who we truly are and make each day a source of wonder. Come with me and discover how to perform this alchemy of the heart.

I have been preparing for a lifetime to take you on this journey. Let me share some of my own story by way of introduction. My life is dedicated to the Earth and all beings that live upon her. For a long time I practiced as an environmental lawyer, bringing federal cases against some of the most powerful corporations in America and beating them every time. My cases were always meant to make corporations and the government feel the need to take care of the Earth on their own. At the same time as I was fighting in court, I was confused about who I was, and hungry with hope that we could find a better way to live. I began to investigate spiritual practice. I studied Zen with a master in Los Angeles called Taizan Maezumi Roshi. Once I got the taste for Zen, I studied with him until his death ten years later.

With his encouragement, I followed the roots of Zen back into Hinduism. I moved to Germany, and lived and studied with a great Hindu master called Mother Meera. The fourteen months of retreat I spent with her were the most revelatory time of my life.

These two great teachers helped me enter the realm of the soul. It was the realm they knew, and a realm we all can know. Through practice, this realm of the soul became my ordinary life. My teachers then encouraged me to share my understanding with you by writing this book.

A third great master, the Dalai Lama, also played a central role. I made a pilgrimage to Dharamsala, India, to ask the Dalai Lama how to bring spiritual and environmental practice together. Since that time, I have made every effort to follow his counsel so that we can all live more harmoniously with each other and the Earth.

From Maezumi Roshi I learned the way of the mind. From Mother Meera I learned the way of the heart. From the Dalai Lama I learned the way of action. As my experience of the soul deepened, the Christianity of my youth opened to me again more fully than I would have thought possible. Letting myself be swept away in the three great rivers of Buddhism, Hinduism, and Christianity, I have been returned to the Source, the great ocean of truth lying undiscovered before me. I want to share the excitement and wonder of this homecoming with you, so that you may make it your own.

When a bear hibernates, its full powers are put aside for a while. But when it awakens, awakens slowly to the inviting rhythms of spring, its powers return and flow full force again. The bear stretches, moves out of its den into the sunshine, and feels the Earth once more. It walks off to feed, experience bearness, and revel in it. We are like the bear. We slumber, while all our strength awaits the moment of awakening. That time is ours to decide. It is we who call spring to our inner landscape. When we call, this inner spring must come. And then—ah!—what a joy to stretch and scratch and leave the darkness of our winter's den! If a hard-nosed, workaholic federal court litigator can do this, so can we all.

Listening to the Landscape

When we walk through a landscape we first notice the obvious features, the lay of the land, woods, streams. The next time we notice more. We may begin to observe how the land lies in relation to more distant landforms. We may begin to see individual trees. As we return, we may sense that we have crossed into the territory of a red-tailed hawk and that the same golden orbweb spider is repairing her net every evening in the same spot, a good flyway for nocturnal insects.

We begin to notice that there are a great many mushrooms on that one hill. One day we find thirty-six mushroom species on a single walk in spring. We observe how the seasons bring change, and over time, how the years each have a different mood. As we return to the same landscape over a period of years, it not only discloses itself more and more, but it begins to mirror who we are. Paintings can be mirrors too. As a boy I was fascinated by Dürer's self-portrait. As I go through life, that portrait is a mirror. Remembering my reactions to it at six years old, I can experience the change in myself in the intervening years by noticing how much Dürer seems to have changed.

As we become more familiar with a landscape, we begin to penetrate into cycles of its life. We see things on both a smaller and a larger scale. We experience the life of individual insects, and the state of the landscape as a whole. We begin to be not a visitor entering the landscape but a participant, in deep conversation with it, listening to the language of the mosses, the language of the pines, the language of the birds, mammals, reptiles, and insects. As we listen to these languages we learn about ourselves. Our perception becomes subtler, and we have moments of thinking like a butterfly, like a wren, like a grove of aspen.

One late afternoon, we will see in the golden light of summer an emergence of crane flies. Listen to their language. Like enormous spindly mosquitoes interested in plants instead of us, the gold-amber crane flies emerge in lumbering flight in their thousands, looking for mates to carry on crane fly kind. If we are listening to the language of the crane flies, we will experience a rapturous wonder at the richness of life. The glorious warmth of coming to be, the in-placeness of finding ourselves part of a slowly swarming throng. We might have missed the miracle of the crane flies if we had not slowed down to the rhythms of the real.

The word *naturalist* is an old-fashioned word. In Darwin's day, it was possible to be a professional naturalist. No longer. Knowledge has fractured into specialties, each with its own mysteries. Nowadays there are only amateur naturalists. With the notion of amateur comes the freedom that experts lose, the freedom to admit ignorance, the freedom to learn.

The word *naturalist* is now, and has always been, a kind of blind to hide behind. The naturalist is a passionately keen lover out to know everything about the beloved. There is no look, gesture, or mood, nothing mundane, no biological function, that does not reduce the naturalist to reverie. The same can be true of the modern specialist. A man can claim to be studying ants and can hide amatory obsession behind erudite taxonomy. He can be a lover out to absorb the teachings of the beloved. It is love that carries us into knowledge, love that pulls us into life. Where our attention goes our love goes.

As a little boy I did not need to hide behind a screen of any kind in loving the natural world, for little boys are allowed to do what I did: hunt for snakes, breed tarantulas and black widows, watch birds without apology. As a boy I would wake up and ask what wonder, what miracle of life, each day would disclose.

I have been studying the inner landscape with the eye of a naturalist for many years now. I was driven to it in desperation, for life made no sense at a certain point, and I needed to know why I was alive. The question "Who am I?" became my only concern. Coming to know ourselves is like learning the language of life in the landscape. We know who we are by searching the inner landscape—the inscape—and emerging into the real. Although it is often desperation that drives the search, if we persist we will discover the lover's regard for the miracle of who we are.

A few years ago, in a small village in Germany, I woke up one morning and realized that the child's sense of wonder had returned. I had been given the grace to feel, viscerally, that the day would disclose wonders. Wonders of consciousness, wonders of the heart, wonders about the relation of mind to feeling, wonders about the interdependence of this awareness and the rest of the Universe. Wonders of being able to see into the suffering of others and touch them with love. Once this wonder is ignited, or reignited, there is no end to it.

Be careful. If you let yourself feel this wonder, you will be lost. You will never get over it. It will become the center of your life. The consequences will be dramatic, and you risk being labeled an eccentric by your fellow humans: life will begin to make sense; meaning will come into your life unbidden; doubt will drop away and you will know who you are.

A Voice in the Wilderness

As we set off consciously on the journey of our life, we carry our story with us. In my case, after studying Zen for eight years or so, I felt the need to go much deeper. During those years I had established the Los Angeles office of the national environmental organization where I worked as an attorney. It was exhausting work. I was slowly and with much regret coming to the conclusion that even if all our efforts succeeded, we would not resolve the disharmony in our society that would tear the Earth and ourselves apart. The dawning of this feeling was something I resisted, since it seemed to challenge everything I had spent my professional life working on. Where would the vision come from of how to live in harmony with the Earth?

I found the beginning of a vision in a Native American sweat lodge. The man leading the ceremony spoke not in the abstraction of Western theology, nor of the emptiness of the East. He spoke only of the natural world, of our relationship with all living things and with the Earth. "This is how I feel," I thought, sitting there as a burned-out environmental lawyer. "Why have I never realized this intimacy with the Earth is real spirituality?"

I felt at home in the sweat lodge, in the dark, in the heat, reentering a sacred womb to reconnect with the Earth. After a long time, the leader suggested that we go around the lodge and each person offer a prayer.

I was sure that I would not participate. I had not prayed since I was a boy, and had left Catholicism, but as my turn approached, I decided I would say whatever came out of my heart. And it was this: "O Great Spirit, let us not cut down the forests in our hearts, out of fear of the beasts that dwell in them."

I was surprised by these words and did not know how to understand them. So I let them rest in my heart.

After a certain time in Los Angeles, the need to go deeper could no longer be postponed. My Zen practice was on a plateau, and I was exhausted from work. I had not understood who I was, and felt the pressure of time to do so. I decided to take an eight-day solo backpack in the High Sierras. I had no clear idea of what I wanted, apart from feeling the need for clarification of my life. Before going, I sat with a friend, a man of some importance in Los Angeles, in a restaurant he owned where media moguls make deals as they dine. I said I was going into the mountains alone for eight days.

"Why are you going?" my friend asked.

"To find God," I answered, much to my own astonishment. I had certainly never put it to myself that way. I was sure I did not believe in anything that could be called God. A gift of Zen is that you can experience the sacred with no talk of God.

"Will you take dried food?" my friend asked, perhaps also astonished. Perfect response from a restaurateur.

I headed up to the Rae Lakes region. The first four days were agonizing, since I wanted to cover some distance and was in terrible shape. On the fifth day I came to a lake just short of the tree line. It was clear enough to see the trout swimming in the cold waters below, and I decided to spend a day there.

I made camp and sat on a ridge nearby, at the base of a

hill. Dusk found me reading David Bohm's dialogue with Krishnamurti called *The Ending of Time*. Absorbed in reading, I was startled when a coyote ran down the hill toward me. He was clearly taken aback to find me there. I was sitting on a path he must have taken in the evenings. I looked at him, and he backed off and went around me.

I spent the next day just looking, a day of deep regard for things. I would find a spot to sit by the lake and just look out for hours at a time, giving my attention to whatever was before me, returning my mind always to the present, to my breath, to what was in front of my eyes. I practiced being fully present in the landscape.

At dusk I stood in my camp, near where I had seen the coyote the day before. He again ran down the hill. Again right at me. This time he was annoyed and I was equally annoyed. I decided he had to know that. I jumped. He jumped. I jumped twice. He jumped twice. "So this is what hopping mad is!" I thought, delighted.

I jumped three times, and he started to come on, snarling. I picked up a stone and threw it at him. We were having a conversation about territory. He was getting it back in a day, but I did not intend to be chased off. He retreated and again went around me.

That night the Moon was full. I felt free after my day of regarding things. Emptied out, relaxed. I found a flat piece of granite polished smooth by glaciers, a white mirror in a meadow in the moonlight. I danced by the light of the Moon. For my freedom, for all the people of my country, I danced.

The next morning I had finished my muesli and the strong coffee brewed on my portable stove. I stood looking up at the mountains, and I heard a voice. I had never heard a voice before, only the natterings of my own mind. This voice boomed out into the valley and was clearly masculine, and the experience of the Old Testament Jews suddenly made sense to me.

It said, "Do you have the courage for the solitude you need to face those beasts?" I knew the voice referred to the prayer I had made in the sweat lodge. The beasts in the forests of my heart.

I was shattered. I was being listened to by a force much greater than my own mind. I was deeply regarded by it, thoroughly known. And not only that. This was not some distant, ephemeral entity. It was speaking in a voice that filled the valley. Whatever it was had penetrated my phenomenological space.

I found myself crying with happiness, weeping away separateness. All I had ever wanted to do was face those beasts and know who I am. Whatever power now spoke supported me in that. Compromise was ruled out and no longer appropriate.

Weeping, I answered, "Do I have any choice?" laughing, knowing that there was only one choice for me.

After a time, the physical and emotional exaltation was enough. I staggered over to a tree that I had gotten to know the day before and held on to it, knowing that it would ground me by letting the excess excitement run into the Earth.

I sat down and took stock of my life. I knew that I had to leave my job. I realized that I had founded the environmental law office not to continue my career as a litigator but as a way of taking care of the environment in Southern California. It had a wonderful staff and would survive as a healthy organism without me. Without knowing where it would lead, I decided to take a year and concentrate full-time on finding out who I was. I had to make time for the solitude the voice spoke of. In that solitude, the beasts would come, and I would face them.

Absolute Sincerity

The day I heard the voice, I spent more time in deep regard for things. I moved on to the next lake and watched the trout, long and fat, and entered into the feel of their swimming, deep and green. I experienced the Sun's light move across the mountains, and wondered what the mountains had to teach me. Watched the scintillation of the sunlight on the surface of the lake. That afternoon, those beats of the sun were gateways through which I moved between levels of awareness.

I took time to pick up and rebury toilet paper, spoor of previous campers, scattered about the area in which the voice had chosen to speak to me. I cleaned up the sacred grove. A whole day of quiet time, simple time, sacred time. Time to walk the landscape of my heart and mind. Time to begin my life's work.

The day after, I was to walk over a pass above the tree line and down a valley that would return me by a circular route to where I had started out, because I hate to backtrack. As I hiked into the granite scree of the pass, I kept pausing to let in what was there. Nothing rapturous at this point, just the recognition that I needed to be slow, to let myself be dissolved into the spirit of the place. And to let the spirit of the place, its elements undefinable, enter into me. As I climbed higher the land became fully alpine. I often paused to study the plants. Small miracles of adaptation, green plants growing on bare rock above the tree line, blooming their life forward through the brief mountain summer. Plants fully articulated and mature the size of a dime, with complex flowers no bigger than a matchhead. In the desert, living things tend to be outsized; in the alpine zone miniature. Bending to see them, I asked them to teach me lessons of endurance.

Over the pass, I walked down the valley, arms open wide like Bellini's St. Francis, consciously thanking all the beings in the mountains for having taken such good care of me and treating me with such intimacy.

It was then the voice returned, once more filling the valley. It said, "You must take this [experience] out [to the world] with absolute sincerity."

I was not comfortable with this, and tried to reason with it. I said, "You know what it's like out there. There are organizations, funders to please, and so on. Half of me will be absolutely sincere; the other half will have to speak in the ways they understand."

"No!" it said. "I mean ABSOLUTE sincerity."

I was again elevated and shattered. I wept as I walked, not knowing how I could do this, or even sure what absolute sincerity was. I walked on to a cataract. The rushing stream of snowmelt that had sculpted the valley there dives over a collection of large polished black stones, gneisslike. Still crying, I stopped at the cataract. I addressed it and said, "Brother, what does it mean, this absolute sincerity?"

The cataract replied. Its voice was different from the voice that had spoken earlier. It did not fill the valley with the very authority that had made the valley. It was a smaller, hushed, more intimate voice. Nevertheless, it spoke, and that day I was given ears to hear.

The cataract said:

I think neither of yesterday,
today, nor tomorrow.
When the snows are great
I am great.
When the snows are small,
I am small.
These rocks take a very long
time to wash away.

"Thank you, Brother!" I laughed, a little dizzy with the depth of the understanding of sincerity the cataract shared so well. Its teaching was clear, and brought me back to myself. I would have to find the patience of the cataract. I would have to do my task with an equal economy of resources, an equal humility. I would have to give up my notion of the pace at which things in my culture should change. The cataract was the clearest demonstration of sincerity I could have been given.

All I had to do was ask. It was clear that I was being given whatever I needed. The issue now was trust.

An Invitation

I invite you now to come with me on your own hero's journey. By embarking on this journey we invite the soul forward. It will come, and we will become intimate with it. This is something we will never regret, even for a moment.

We begin our journey at the edge of the old wisdoms and what they can do for us. All the problems that threaten social dissolution—from declining respect for government, to crime and drug use, to overpopulation, unemployment, environmental degradation, the collapse of authority in central Africa, and all the rest—have a single root. The old stories no longer inspire us to find personal clarity or social cohesion. We need a new wisdom.

This should not surprise us. We have reached a threshold of human evolutionary change. Within the last fifty years, we have gone from being a species with mostly local influence to the one that dominates life on the globe. As yet we have made no shift in consciousness consonant with our shift in status. It is not that technological humankind has fallen from grace or forgotten a wisdom we once had. The lesson is more humbling and less romantic: we are still primitive, still acting as biomass. We humans have never yet risen from the primal urge to consume resources, the urge that drives every species that we believe to be inferior to ourselves.

Like any other species, we have begun to run into the limiting wisdom of the Earth. We can expect to be put in our place by the traditional methods raised to a global pitch: plagues, famines, ecodisasters, all visited disproportionately on the weak rather than the strong.

Our challenge is not to find old wisdom we have forgotten or failed to apply vigorously enough. Our challenge is to grow into a new wisdom that we have never had, to embody the wisdom of the Earth until there is no way we can act except in harmony with the Earth. To apply the wisdom of the Earth through ourselves, rather than suffer its application to us.

Traditional religions do not offer real guidance. None of them has kept any modern nation from acting toward either the Earth or its own people like every other one. Perhaps this is because the great religions come from earlier times when human actions did not have such an impact on the entire globe.

Where, then, can we turn? The tools of reason and analysis alone are not sufficient, because they will never move us deeply enough. We need to enter into a new consciousness, one befitting our new status as *the* dominant global species. For this we need a new story.

We need a story that relates human life to the entire living Earth and to the cosmos, and gives us a pedagogical way to follow from childhood into maturity, gaining wisdom as we go. We also need a practical method of applying the perspective in this new story to everyday life, a way of remembering who we are in the midst of life's growing complexities, and a way of accentuating the positive when it eludes us.

We each need to awaken to this new story. A new human wisdom, a global wisdom, will emerge out of individual awakenings if enough of us awaken. Let us awaken now together, for the sake of all that lives.

· · ·

This book will show you how to experience your own mind, heart, and action. It provides field marks to help you understand your evolving experience and is designed for busy people living in the world with all the commitments of work and family. The book offers a way to awaken that opens us to the sacred character of our daily experience. We are both ape and angel, and so all of human life is included in our practice. Nothing that is human is outside it.

The book provides a set of exercises that allow you to work safely with all the difficult and painful material in your life. As you do these exercises, you will come to know the joyful, spontaneous being that you truly are. The book is laid out as a journey through the inner landscape, for this is how we come to know the soul. Each of us will find his or her own path for this journey, as we explore the three great ways of awakening:

- The Way of the Mind
- The Way of the Heart
- The Way of Action

In **The Way of the Mind**, we enter into deep inner silence and learn how to bring our analytic mind along on our journey. We discover all the tools that we need to find out who we truly are, and we experiment with them. We learn, too, how inner silence sheds stress and lets us summon our deepest creativity at will.

In **The Way of the Heart**, we learn to focus our emotional being so that when we cry out to Heaven, we know ourselves heard and feel ourselves answered. We move through a series of exercises on how to offer our life to the Divine from the moment we wake in the morning until we go to sleep at night. We walk into the forests of our hearts and meet the beasts that dwell in them. We learn how to release these beasts and thereby liberate ourselves. We then investigate praise and enter the deep, sweet ravishment that only the mystics know.

In **The Way of Action,** we focus on our work in the world. We learn to concentrate on our actions and release their fruits. We see what it is that we really need from the world and gain clarity about what we live for. We discover a radical confidence that remains, even when chaos seems to swirl around us.

We then explore our connection with the natural world. So intimately do we experience it that we begin to see our inner landscape and the outer landscape as twin aspects of a single reality. Finally, we explore the implications of the Gaia hypothesis—which sees the whole Earth as a single living entity—for our own life and story.

This is a rough overview of our journey. We will take it step by step. Remember always to go at your own pace. Do the exercises in a way that feels right, but also push yourself a little. Use this book to grow.

And please make this book your own. Keep it near you, and refer to it when you need it. Scribble notes in it, fill it with vining marginalia, put a waterproof cover on it, do whatever you need to make it your familiar. When you make it your own, it will provide you with answers when you need them.

2

On the
Threshold
of the Soulpaths

What Do We Trust?

In what do we place our trust? Do we trust in something? If we were medieval Europeans, we would trust in a Divine Providence. In our time, there is a deep nostalgia for belief, a longing to trust. Let us consider what we might trust in all aspects of our lives.

Our democratic tradition asks us to trust in a government that will promote our welfare, securing our liberties so that we can work toward happiness. Do we trust in government to promote our welfare?

The power of national governments has now been exceeded in many respects by multinational corporations. These are a new kind of global entity, a privately controlled form of government unprecedented in its ability to consume resources and affect people's lives. Do we trust them?

Do we feel that the Universe is a friendly place or an unfriendly one? A place hospitable to our needs? Do we believe in a beneficent power? A reality, however described, that we can rely on and perhaps know intimately? Do we trust the Universe to provide the opportunities we need to live life fully?

Perhaps we place no final trust in external forces or institutions. Do we nevertheless trust other human beings? Do we place our trust in a lover, a guru, a parent or child, or in some other person we are in a relationship with?

Do we trust in our own abilities? In our own pluckiness, our power to make our way in a seemingly hostile world, carving out a niche to meet our needs while our strength holds out?

Where do we place our trust? If we have put it in government or corporations, we will have been disabused. Perhaps we were told it was safe to eat beef with Creutzfeld-Jacob disease and believed it, or believed that cigarettes were not addictive.

Every time we see or hear an advertisement, we soak in an unspoken, corrosive message: we are not valuable in ourselves, we cannot be fulfilled, we have no purpose or meaning until we buy the next product. This is the central mantra of our culture, droning on with much greater devotion than *Om* was ever chanted in India: "Buy this and you will be happy; when not consuming you have no reason for existence."

A time will come, if we are paying attention, when we will see through our culture. We will see that as a race we are ravaging the ancient, complex web of life on Earth, destroying the wisdom encoded in billions of years of life's blossoming forth. All for no good reason.

If we have placed our trust in human beings, we will have known betrayal, loss, disappointment. If we look to other people to make us happy, a time will come when we will realize that no one but ourselves can ever make us happy. This is a difficult lesson to learn, and we are very resistant to learning it.

What do we do when we realize these kinds of things? Do we become discouraged and cynical? Or do we have a way of facing all the darkness in our life, all the shadows in our inner landscape, and walking through them? A way that does not use fake hope to dull our pain, fake nirvanas to dull our intellects, fake promises to dull our understanding of the world's ills?

Do we trust in anything? The need to trust is as deep a human need as the needs for food, sex, and a sense of accomplishment. We need to trust; trust begins to ease the pain we feel when we see through our culture. It gives us room to end our alienation and despair, our cynicism and disillusionment.

Ultimately, we must learn to trust ourselves. When we do this intimately and intelligently, the world opens full of meaning before us. We find that we ourselves are the doorway to a fathomless understanding of the source of life itself. We need only learn how to walk through it.

Yet we cannot move from alienation, disillusionment, cynicism, and despair to trust in ourselves all in one go. Nor can we accomplish it by mental resolve alone. It is a process that takes time and attention. Our journey together is a sequence of experiments in a growing intimacy with the source of wisdom within ourselves.

But first a story. When Aristotle defined human beings as rational animals, he was forgetting about stories. We need stories, especially foundational stories that spell out who we are as human beings on the Earth. In all cultures throughout all time, human beings have used stories to situate themselves in a stream of meaning. We use them to give us maps out of chaos and clues to wisdom.

In our culture, we lack such a story. For many of us, Genesis is now a story that must be explained so that it fits our view of the world, rather than a story that makes sense of the world. It may even seem quaint, as remote from our perceptions as an origin myth from a South Sea Island tribe. Although we lack any explicit story of our origins, we have a tacit one. It filters into the background of our awareness and shapes our view of ourselves. It is more likely to teach us self-loathing than any wicked stepmother could have done. Our origin story is a product of the failure of institutional religion, the mechanistic view of mainstream science, and the ascendancy of unalloyed materialism. It goes roughly like this:

> The Universe was created out of nothing by no one for no reason at all. Life appeared because of random processes, and could just as well not have done so. Once life appeared, it flourished because conditions were accidentally right for it to do so. Despite all human striving, life has no meaning except to consume resources and relationships for whatever passing palliation they can give. We have not been equipped by evolution with the tools to solve the global problems we have caused. We will probably destroy ourselves and much or all of life on Earth in the next hundred years, if not sooner. The dinosaurs came and went and so shall we, but that is just the tough game of evolution in an empty and mechanical Universe.

This kind of story is a no-exit nightmare of nihilism. But is it not close to the story our culture gives us? Isn't this why, ultimately, we are faced with a growing fear of social dissolution?

Our culture has lost touch with the soul and with any way to meet it. It becomes more difficult all the time simply to be quiet: mobile phones, faxes, and E-mail make us more accessible to the intrusion of information. Being reflective may soon seem a radical act. Without being reflective, without entering into moments of silence, we cannot let the soul in. The soul's voice is a still, soft one, and we must be quiet if we are to hear it.

Let us begin our journey with a bold experiment:

Begin with the nihilistic story above. Take the time to imagine what the world would be like if all the terms of this story were changed. Go through the paragraph one sentence at a time, and imagine a thoroughly positive version of the story.

Take some time with this reflective exercise. Do it when you are alone and quiet, when you are in the country, or taking a walk in a city park. Perhaps you want to take a long hot bath with it.

Let your imagination run completely free. Your story can be as wild and rich as you want. We can make myths that fit both the yearnings of the heart and what we know of science. Tell yourself whatever story comes to you, taking all the time you need.

Then write it down. Give it the shape of written language. Illustrate it if you want. Hold on to it. This is the beginning of a personal genesis story that will grow slowly in your heart now that you have planted the seeds.

You may want to look at your story again after you have worked with the practices outlined in this book. It's likely your view will evolve as you make the practices your own and use them on your path.

My own Genesis story started that day in the High Sierras. I offer it not to supplant your story but to strike flint, start sparks, and perhaps enrich your own. This is the first foray on our journey into a story that makes sense of our lives by situating them in a universal process. Such a story is a real myth, vital and living. Such a myth underlies and supports our practice. As we proceed on our journey, we will find the seeds of a new myth within our own experience. Before we go further, though, a word on science. Science is one of the glories of our world. It is the work of the analytic mind in love with life, and its poetry is mathematics. Science continuously reveals wonder, if we let it, and seamlessly meets the experiences we find on a soulpath. Nothing of science need be remote from us; the more we know physical reality the more we know ourselves.

Moreover, all vital myth, whether for the Greeks, for indigenous peoples, or for ourselves, uses the best science of its day. If it does not weave the sharpest understanding of the world into a pattern of meaning, it does not live.

So here is a Genesis story:

In the beginning was the Plenum, the ocean of energy in which all Universes lie enfolded. Energies beyond measure moved as waves within the Plenum as easily as waves of thought. And then in a moment of silence before time, a myriad of these waves met, erupted into light, and so our Universe was born.

The light moved and its movement made space; and its movement through space made time. Light's movement diverged as it flowed, and moved into harmonics of itself.

The lower register slowed into gas. The higher remained consciousness, as it always was. The gas collected into stars, which ignited when they became dense enough to do so. The burning of stars made all the other kinds of matter. As they burned for billions of years, stars made everything there is out of the original gas. They made all the ingredients of life in their fiery hearts.

Everything we are was made for us by stars, and so we are the children of stars: our bones' calcium was made in stars; our skin's carbon was made in stars; it was stars that made the iron that lets our blood flow red and brings oxygen to our cells.

To make the iron on which our life depends, stars

sacrificed themselves. Because iron is so heavy, the stars that made it imploded in upon themselves. Blossoming then in great thermonuclear novas, they made yet heavier matter as they exploded, and seeded the Universe with all the ingredients of life.

Some of this star matter collected around new stars and, cooling, formed planets. The planets were made of everything needed for life. And life emerged as soon as hospitable planets cooled. Life emerged because it had to bloom, encoded as it was in the structure of matter itself. It emerged many times on many planets.

When life began on Earth, everything was red. All the oxygen we breathe was bound up in rocks, and everything looked rusty. Even the sky was red. The first cells lived simply in this world for more than a billion years. Then a cell began to free the oxygen. It used it as a poison, to increase its domain, for the other cells could not stand it. Soon other cells began to release oxygen too, and the sky became blue for the first time.

As soon as life covered Earth, Gaia was born. Gaia emerged already a superorganism, the conscious life of Earth. She made the air and water and temperature all fit for life to thrive. As soon as Gaia was born, life indeed did thrive.

Plants began to make food from the light of the Sun. Soon the oceans and then the land teemed with animals and plants. Oxygen became so abundant for a time that life took on huge shapes, from dinosaurs to dragonflies big as eagles.

As all these forms of life emerged, Gaia shared her consciousness with them, and there was no separation between the consciousness of living things and that of Gaia. In Gaia and her creatures, consciousness and matter work for complete union, in which matter can come wholly into consciousness, and consciousness wholly into matter.

Self-consciousness in Gaia came alive in humans. We were not always self-aware. It happened long ago, when we lived in caves. Caves were cold and dark and sometimes concealed terrifying things like bears.

One day, lightning struck a dead tree near the opening to our cave. The tree caught fire and burned. One of us, watching, touched the fire with a dry stick, and it became a burning brand. We gathered more dry sticks and brought the fire home.

We sat around the fire, warm and grateful. It was then the thought arose, "We did this!" For each of us, the next thought was "I did this!" This "I" ignited, burned brighter than the fire, and has been burning ever since.

Soon we painted scenes on the walls of the caves by torchlight. Scenes of bison and reindeer, aurochs, ibex, and rhino. A good time to be alive.

Something else began to happen. When we listened to birdcalls, we became wistful. The nightingale reminded us of last summer's love, now long gone. We began to feel lonely and separate.

This separation reflects the original separation between light and matter. Just as we yearn to heal our separation, matter and light yearn to heal their separation through us.

Feeling separate, we came upon anger and avarice, the dark passions of matter as it moves toward light. Allowing ourselves to be possessed by these, we try to make ourselves great at the expense of Gaia, and so approach the edge of self-destruction.

Yet within separation lies the hope of return. For when human beings open mind and heart, we are a doorway through which the impassioned shadows cast by matter can reach light, and light can penetrate these shadows.

This does not happen on its own. Only we can open our mind and heart. The time to do so is upon us: we are poised on a cusp of human evolution. Gaia has begun to call us into an awakening. An awakening as human beings and as the human race. An awakening into intimacy with ourselves and with the Earth at last. An awakening into the ongoing miracle of life.

It is a wonderful call, and we and Gaia will grow and change together if we heed it. Let us hear it and follow. For the other way lies madness, and certain widespread death.

Questions at the Threshold

Let us move now to the personal, to questions at the threshold of our practice. Until we raise them for ourselves and answer them, we may think about crossing the threshold but will never succeed in doing so.

The questions at the threshold are two:

Am I willing to let go of all my suffering and all my
    familiar dramas?
Am I willing to be happy?

Beyond Suffering

Suffering has another side, the side we look back on after we have been through it. On the other side of suffering is radical confidence. To come to radical confidence is like finding an enclosed garden planted with roses after crossing the desert on foot. The ancient Persian word for *garden* is the root of our word *paradise*. To have traversed suffering on foot, and come to a place where joy flowers, is like finding oneself in paradise.

We are both desert and garden, and need only remember how to enter the garden. The key to the garden is fashioned by a choice that is ours to make. To enter, we must choose to unclutch our suffering. Suffering is different from pain. If we have grief, toothache, or a wound, what we have is pain. If we elaborate on it, nurture it, hold on to it, we turn it into suffering. We get plenty of pain by living in a body. Yet we often add suffering to our pain. Are we ready to live without suffering?

Few of us are. Most of us clutch our suffering close and think it the most important thing about us. It is all we want to tell people about ourselves. Why? Suffering resolves all doubts. It gives us a job in life, something to do while we are waiting to die. Our suffering is what we know; it is our familiar funk. Suffering is our drama, and we put everything we have into our drama. It is what we gossip about. It is what we think interesting. It is what we use all our lives long to distract us from facing the reality of who we are. Do we want to know ourselves enough to give up our drama?

The drama of our suffering is a map that gives a name and a place to every feature in our inner landscape. It lies close in our darkness and whispers words of comfort, though the comfort is pernicious and cold. The price of this familiarity is high. We wind up adopting the viewpoint of our suffering, taking our drama to be real, renouncing hope, and forgetting we have done so. We stay in the desert, denying there is a way out and saying that only fools believe in gardens. We prefer suffering's cold comfort over the water and roses of paradise. Are we not very like Shaw's Don Juan in *Don Juan in Hell*, afraid that if we let our drama go we will become beatific but bored? Why do we think our endlessly improvised drama of suffering is interesting?

Once we have entered the garden we know it is real. If we find ourselves in the desert again—and the nature of our journey, like climbing a spiral staircase, so that we meet similar material raised to higher levels, makes this likely—it will be less daunting. We realize we have been through it before, and so we know we can do it again.

We should remember, however, that entering the garden is not without risks. If we unclutch our suffering, we lose the map of who we think we are. We will have to be prepared for finding out things about ourselves that our suffering distracted us from. We will lose the intense, turbulent drama we adore. We will need to be ready to find another way to live.

Are You Happy?

And now the second threshold question: Are you happy? When we ask this question with penetrating honesty, we find out where we are in our life.

It is hard to ask this question with absolute sincerity. For years, every time I asked it, I answered quickly: "Yes! I am happy!" I used vigor and speed to cut off inner conversation, making myself into an old-style Soviet commissar standing between me and the true answer.

Are you happy? Ask yourself the question, but be gentle with yourself about answering it. Let it be an open question. No one else need know the answer. The question may take time to answer, for it is an ultimate question. Give yourself the freedom to allow any answer to emerge. When you do this you are already touching the source of happiness, since you are giving yourself permission to touch the truth. If you can trust yourself in this way, you have already moved into an ultimate resolution of the question.

Here is a story:

A beggar lived next to an open sewer. The sewer stank horribly day and night, attracting rats and hordes of flies. One day a rich man came along and took pity on the beggar. He moved him into a beautiful new house.

The house had a spacious courtyard with a fountain that gushed pure, clean water. There was a bedroom with a wonderful bed and clean new sheets. The rich man also gave the beggar a substantial sum of money, so that he could buy whatever else he needed to make himself happy.

The beggar lived in the wonderful new house but felt miserable. He was puzzled as to why he could feel miserable in such a fine place. Then he realized what he needed. He immediately hired several workmen to take out the fountain in the courtyard and replace it with an open sewer, complete with the contents of the sewer he used to live next to, and plenty of rats and flies. He had his bed moved out into the courtyard and slept next to the sewer.

The rich man came by to check on him and was horrified. "Why have you done this to the beautiful house I gave you?" he asked.

"Isn't it wonderful?" the beggar said proudly. "Now it looks and smells like home!"

Are you happy? Try a simple experiment.

Sit quietly and relax your body and mind. Sit for five minutes, relaxing.

Are you happy? Watch where your thoughts go. What comes into your mind in response to the question?

Watch your thoughts for just five minutes. What arises in your mind that gives you satisfaction? What that brings you frustration? Are you too agitated to be able to watch your thoughts at all?

When you are ready to move on, try a second question.

Do you believe that you deserve to be happy? Are you really sure that you merit happiness? Take a second five minutes and sit with this question. What arises?

Many people tell me that they do not deserve to be happy. They are almost offended, and may become angry, when told they have a right to be happy. What do you believe?

What do I mean by happiness? What is the happiness that I am suggesting is the birthright of every one of us? Let me first say what it is not. It is not an emotional high, the kind of feeling we get when our bloodstream is full of the chemicals we make as we fall in love. As we know from experience, this kind of feeling is ephemeral. Nor does the happiness I am talking about result from what ads say makes us happy: material things, money, sex, and all the rest.

The happiness I am talking about is more profound than all of these. It is an inner balance and poise, an awareness of our own center of gravity. It is not something that comes and goes, as all feelings do by their very nature. It is instead a state of being. Of being in touch with ourselves, whatever is happening around us. Of being able to know our own mind and heart, our own needs, no matter how loud the clamor gets. The happiness that our culture asks us to strive for is a flimsy thing, a momentary reaction to passing circumstance. If we try to make ourselves happy by the method our culture suggests, we will doom ourselves to dependence on circumstances we can never control.

Real happiness is largely independent of circumstances. It lies in our relationship to them. It derives from and resides in a certain positive stance to all the circumstances we meet. It is what makes us independent. It is what makes people dying of AIDS or cancer able to appreciate life deeply even as their energies wane.

Let us not put this happiness aside, thinking it is selfish. If we say that we do not deserve to be happy while others go hungry, how will we ever find the strength to help them? Let us be careful not to find high-minded reasons to cling to our own suffering. It is from our own real happiness that we can best work to alleviate the suffering of others.

When we ask these questions in an absolutely sincere way, without forcing the answer, we begin to live them. We begin to inquire into who we really are. As we live these questions, we become an artist of our own life. Everything we meet in life opens us to aspects of our answer.

We need to understand that we are inherently perfect and that we have details to work out. If we lose sight of the fact that we are inherently perfect, we can become lost in self-help programs, convinced that we are just an endless set of problems. Or worse, we can become convinced that the existentialists were right and that we live in a meaningless Universe. Though inherently perfect, we also have details to work out; this is why we take up spiritual practice.

Happiness is our birthright. It is also a decision we have to make: we will not be happy unless we consciously choose to be happy. I first heard this notion some years ago from the Dalai Lama. My reaction was a strong one: "This guy is a moron!" I thought. "I'm not happy, and there are plenty of good reasons for my unhappiness external to myself!" It took me years to decide that it would not hurt me to experiment and see if he was right. This is an experiment we can all make.

If you have answered the threshold questions about suffering and happiness for yourself, we can begin to inquire together into what a soulpath is. People never awaken until they tire of their drama. If your drama excites you and you want to hold on to it, that is your choice. No one else can force you to let go of it. If you want your drama, put this book down now. Go off and enjoy the drama, but do not pretend that you are doing anything else. Otherwise you will confuse yourself, using the language and practice of a soulpath as just another venue for your drama. Ultimately, the choice is an absolutely clear one for each of us to make.

3

A Natural History of the Soul

The Psyche and the Soul

Our journey is about to enter its central passage: the realm of the soul in ordinary life. We need to be clear about what we mean by soul. As used by most contemporary psychologists, the words *psyche* and *soul* are interchangeable. That is not how we will use them.

In our discussion, body, psyche, and soul are three distinct realms. Distinct but interacting, thus: the marriage of body and soul produces psyche. The wedding in human beings of the purely material body and the purely spiritual soul produces the mixed realm of our experience that we call the psyche. The words *psyche, inner landscape,* or *inscape* will all be used to denote this mixed realm. This realm is where we ordinarily locate ourselves. It is what we talk about when we tell stories, what we investigate with our therapists, and where we have dreams. It is also where we have our wounds. It is what most of contemporary psychology is concerned with.

The soul, as we will use the word, is distinct from the psyche. We might think of the soul as an aspect of the Source of All Being localized in space and time. It supports our life, carries our life, is the essence of life itself. The soul is already fully awakened, perfect, always unstained, unborn, and undying. It knows the sacred in everything, for it never loses its perspective.

Although the psyche is full of wounds, full of shadows, rich with darkness, the soul knows no difficulties. We do not need to heal the soul. Indeed, we cannot take care of it. On the contrary, the soul takes care of us. We cannot heal the wounds of the psyche while we remain within the perspective of the psyche. We can heal the psyche only from the perspective of the soul.

As we heal these psychic wounds and let the soul come forward in our life, we experience the soul's spacious view, its serenity, its access to bliss, its wisdom and compassion. As we adopt the soul's perspective, we begin to feel the integral nature of the body, psyche, and soul, and we experience them as three interrelated realms. When we experience this flowing, integral, multidimensional life, we begin to appreciate who we really are.

This use of the word *soul* is related to what the Indian philosophers mean by the Atman; it is related to what the Buddhist psychologists mean by the True Self. We will use the word *soul* because it is a fine Anglo-Saxon word, close to home, warm, familiar, and friendly. If, as you read, you find that the words *soul* and *psyche* have so completely fused for you that this expansive meaning of the word *soul* is uncomfortable, please find your own word. In the end, the journey we are making is beyond all terminologies. We simply need to be clear as we go.

The Intimate Science

What does the soul feel like?

Philosophers and theologians through the ages have inquired into the nature of the soul. The naturalist asks a different question. Of a humbler and homier sort, the naturalist's question is what does the soul feel like? How does it enter into the realm of experience, not of speculation? How can we get to know it in our bones and in our muscle tissues, in our feelings? What difference does it make to our minds and to how our thoughts feel to us?

The next sections of this book detail a set of practices that open us to experiencing the soul. As we do these practices we meet the soul and its movements in our life. We all have the potential to know our soul intimately. It carries our whole life and awaits our invitation. The invitation it responds to takes the form of practice. We feel the soul only when we realize its presence through the receptivity practice brings us. Practice is nothing special; it is only a way of remembering.

We experience the soul coming forward in our lives in a concrete way. We feel it in our thoughts, feelings, actions, and in our bodies. We feel it move from a point behind the heart and become directly involved in our life. The soul will never force itself on us, no matter what the circumstances. It will only come as far forward into our lives as we choose to invite it, as far as we are ready to accept it. When we invite the soul with absolute sincerity, it has no choice but to come forward as far as the life and the invitation permit.

A time comes when, if we allow it to, the soul takes over all aspects of our lives. At this point, no matter what our difficulties may be, we recognize that there is a deep and untroubled stream flowing below all surface troubles and that we are of one substance with that stream. The soul knows no difficulties.

No one else can do this for us. The world does not encourage it. It is too threatening to the world and all its hierarchies. Who can control or manipulate those who have found their freedom? Many will say that this untroubled stream is an illusion or that we are selfish to want to enter it. We can choose to listen to them or we can choose to extend an invitation to our soul.

As the soul comes forward, we begin to identify more with its spaciousness than with the constrictions of the personality we have fashioned for ourselves. This does not mean we lose our individuality, but our various contractions begin to relax, allowing more love through. We will care less for our innumerable grievances and enjoy life more.

The whole point of doing this kind of practice is to gain the wisdom of age while we are still young enough to enjoy it.

Practicing Toward Wisdom

Wisdom is embodied truth, the only kind worth having. It is what remains of our inspirations and mistakes after we have lived them and their results have sifted down into our body, feelings, and intuition. Wisdom is alive and moving, quicker than thought, fresher than words. Wisdom follows from understanding. Then how do we get to understanding? As we grow older we discover the difference between knowledge and understanding. Knowledge takes us only to the threshold. We gain understanding by looking into what causes happiness or pain in the situations that life provides for our tuition. As it accumulates, it coalesces into meaningful patterns.

Wisdom takes time. Time alone, though, is not enough. We can grow old and be as ignorant as we were at the beginning. Wisdom takes practice. The practices that are outlined in the following chapters are wisdom practices. They are also how we study the natural history of the soul. Studying the soul in this way and gaining wisdom are the same endeavor.

As a river ages, it meanders, cutting more curves. If it is forced to flow straight, with the artificial order imposed by engineers, there is no place for the river to deposit sand. When there are bends in the river, the river slows down, and individual grains of sand drop out along a curving bank. Over time, the grains of sand accrete and a sandbar forms. This represents a new level of order and organization.

Wisdom is like that. It accretes slowly, grain by grain. This happens only when the flow of our awareness allows it to. Understanding can drop into our consciousness only if we move slowly enough for it to happen. We need to step aside from the onrushing currents of our thoughts and feelings, and this is not easy to do. Wisdom practices, therefore, take a patient and long-term application.

When uranium atoms are thinly distributed, they give off radiation at a sustained rate, and the story ends there. When a sufficient quantity of them are brought together, however, they stimulate each other. Radiation is released at an increasing rate until there is a chain reaction, which is something different from the behavior of the individual atoms and beyond their capacity. Wisdom is like a chain reaction that happens on its own when enough understanding has accumulated. Wisdom ignites when it is ready, and we realize it only later on, after our perspective has shifted. Wisdom emerges out of understanding, just as Gaia emerged out of life on Earth when life had become vigorous and plentiful enough to cover the globe. By cultivating understanding, we prepare the way for the soul to enter directly into our awareness. We gain access suddenly to a realm of awareness that is at once noncognitive, impersonal, and compassionate.

The method of natural history is a slow and patient process. As naturalists, we put ourselves into intimate contact with what is real, to learn from it patiently. This is true whether we are studying ants in the Amazon or the soul in daily life. Studying the ants, we would learn specific skills of recognition and of physical and mental endurance. We would come to know the open questions in our field and long to answer them, trusting that if we pay attention and let the ants teach us, we will discover things never understood before.

All of this is true when we study the natural history of our own soul. We learn skills and techniques, apply them, and so distinguish features of our own intimate experience we were blind to before. We learn patience and the endurance that comes from needing to know who we are. We collect data, trusting in our methods, revising them, letting our experience teach us. We enter whole realms of understanding that are new. There comes the genuine excitement of discovery and the certainty that our understanding can deepen as long as we are willing to give ourselves to the intoxicating joy of this patient study.

When we study as a naturalist, we do not want to change what we study but to understand it for the sheer love of understanding. What underlies this approach is the intuition that the object of our study, whether the ant or the soul, is a doorway into mystery and perfection, a crystalline point of entry into understanding the whole. When it comes to the soul, the rewards for pursuing this intimate science are happiness, wisdom, and wonder.

Three Ways of the Soul

There are three ways of the soul. The three ways are these: the Way of the Mind, the Way of the Heart, and the Way of Action. Each of these ways has many branches. Just as there are thousands of ways to kneel and kiss the Earth, there are thousands of ways to walk the inscape. In the end, there are as many ways as there are sincere explorers. Each biography is unique, and each heart holds a somewhat different hope.

You can think of the practices that each of these ways offers as a kind of road or trail map. A map of your own inner landscape. A map you consult while on your own hero's journey, for that is what each of our inner journeys truly is. Remember that this guide is meant to be consulted in a way that suits your own very personal journey. Use whatever you find in it that calls to you.

There is no single way best for everyone. The most important thing is to find a way that suits you, that encourages you, that you can follow and make your own.

4

The Way
of the Mind

Introducing the Way

The mind waits to lead us far beyond itself. As we begin the journey, we learn how to live in the present moment, avoiding distraction and shedding stress. Our enjoyment of life deepens and our ability to act coolly under stress sharpens.

When the mind reflects on its source persistently, it goes beyond its identification with particular thoughts and experiences unity. When the mind experiences unity, it remembers that it was never really separate. This remembering changes our experience fundamentally. When the mind is firmly grounded in the experience of unity, the work of integration begins.

The soul is always fully awake. Inviting the soul to come forward into the mind trains us to adopt the soul's wakefulness, until we attain it in all the circumstances of our ordinary life. The way of the mind relies on the fundamental fact that we become whatever we give our attention to.

Goethe said that by middle age we become what we most despise. If we despise something, we have as compelling a relationship with it as if we love it. We think about it constantly, study it, and color it with intense emotion. Without knowing it, we take what we despise into our mind and heart and make it our model. Without seeing what we are doing, we check all our behavior against what we despise. We measure ourselves by it. We make ourselves the victim of what we despise. After years of study, we do, in the end, embody it.

We can also embody what we love. When we let the mind reflect on its source persistently, we begin to do this. We might not feel that we can choose what we turn our minds to. When we experiment with the way our mind works, however, we will see this for ourselves. We have the choice, therefore, of what we become.

The way of the mind trains us to be fully present. Present in the present moment, in the now, in our body, in our feelings, and in our thoughts. Even without going further into awakening, this gives us tremendous power over our experience.

This is why the samurai found the way of the mind appealing and regarded it as a keystone of their skills. How else can we be fully present in the midst of confusion, strife, stress, and difficulty than by training the mind to be present? If the samurai could act calmly in the midst of a battle, he would make the right choices and could command all of his resources and skills. If he were distracted, he would soon be killed.

The way of the mind trains us to remain present in the midst of distractions so that we can make the choices that are appropriate to the moment. If there is stress, we can have the poise to act in the way best calculated to reduce it. If our child or our lover offers us affection, we have the space to receive and acknowledge it. Love is attention. When we are distracted we cannot love.

Training to live in the ensouled mind fundamentally changes our point of view. We do not learn new information or change ourselves. We change our point of view, adopting that of the soul. Once we have done this we can, if we persist, change whatever it is about our habits we need to change.

When we see the ensouled mind in this light, we can drop any fears that we will be asked to kill our ego or lose the use of our analytic faculties. We lose nothing. We shift our point of view, and things fall into their correct perspective for the first time. Our ego is experienced as a useful instrumentality; our analytic faculties as indispensable and enjoyable. We can relax into their use without being tyrannized by them.

Living the Ensouled Mind

The way of the mind begins not in our thoughts but in our bodies. Opening the mind to the wisdom of the body begins a quiet revolution in our moment-to-moment experience. It is the simplest thing we can do. It just takes a willingness to let our mind drop into our body and so return to the present moment again and again. The rewards, in purely pragmatic terms—staying calm and focused in the midst of stressful circumstances—are phenomenal.

Begin the practice like this:

Sit in a comfortable posture, spine straight but not rigid. Sit on a chair, a cushion on the floor, or wherever else you are most comfortable being alert. Relax and feel your body in contact with the Earth. Let yourself feel this contact, whether you are sitting on the grass or in an office in the city. Wherever you are sitting, feel your fundamental contact with the Earth.

Then turn your attention to your breath. In this practice we follow the breath into the body. Genuine transcendence happens in and through the body, not by turning away from it.

Feel the breath in your body. Feel it entering, residing, and leaving. The breath of life, the act of inspira-

tion. *The patient pattern of our body's breath is respiration. Breathing in, we inspire ourselves again. Breathing out, we let all our tension go.*

It happens on its own, just as the beating of our heart happens on its own. Pulsing waves, rising and falling. Our breathing has a deeper rhythm than our mind knows. It is the rhythm of the Earth, filling our lungs. Moving gently and persistently, like waves on the ocean's shore.

Let yourself feel the rhythm of your breath. Let your awareness follow your breath fully. Give your breath your full attention. As you do this, your breath entrains your mind. By turning your awareness to your breath, your mind takes up the rhythm of the breath.

When the mind takes up the rhythm of the breath, it slows down, and distractions gradually begin to fall away. When the awareness follows the breath, the mind comes fully into the present moment. This can happen the first time we sit. It is profoundly refreshing. It is quietly joyful. It is the simplest thing we can do. And we can do it anywhere, anytime.

As distractions begin to fall away from the mind, the mind becomes still and it tastes silence. Let your mind go deeply into silence. We seldom let our minds taste silence. When we do, we wonder why it has taken us so long to do so. Every time we taste it, we wonder this again.

Silence is completely fresh every time. In this silence the sperm whale dives and sounds the ocean's depths. In this silence the Sun pours forth its energy. It is that same silence from which all things emerge. As our inner silence deepens, we come to know the source of our being in direct experience.

When we begin to follow this way, we are opposing the

habits of a lifetime. Because of this, we need to have the ineluctable patience of the cataract that became my teacher in the High Sierras. We need to be patient with ourselves and know that these habits take a very long time to wash away. We may become discouraged when the mind is agitated. We may try to sit in silence and find that the mind wanders again and again into a noisy commerce with our daily concerns. This is perfectly natural. The mind has thoughts. That is what it does, and it will always do it. The Tibetans say that wanting to have a mind without thoughts is like wanting to have meat without bones. Meat comes with bones. Minds come with thoughts.

You cannot force your mind to be silent. Still, it is worth trying, running the experiment for yourself. Try it and see what happens.

You can always, however, gently and persistently, bring the mind back into silence by allowing it to follow the breath. When this is difficult, remember: it is not important how many times your mind strays. What is important is how many times you call it back.

A TAKING REFUGE IN THE PRESENT MOMENT

Before we go further, let us ask a practical question: Without years of practice, how can we find refuge in the present moment when we are upset, distracted, unable to sleep, crazed by worry?

It is very simple.

Follow your breath into your body. Feel your breath. Feel your body. Tell yourself this: "I am here, now, in this body, nowhere else."

Let it sink in. Feel it. Be gentle but firm. Do it. Really do it. No excuses. Simply do it.

When you are troubled by an obsessive thought, follow your breath into your body. Feel your breath. Feel your body. Tell yourself this: "I am here, now, in this body, nowhere else."

When you are agitated, follow your breath into your body. Feel your breath. Feel your body. Tell yourself this: "I am here, now, in this body, nowhere else."

When you are crazed with longing, loneliness, or money problems, when your mind is spinning at a thousand revolutions per second and you want to reach for the painkillers, then follow your breath into your body. Feel your breath. Feel your body. Tell yourself this: "I am here, now, in this body, nowhere else."

Be firm but loving, as if you were training a puppy. When we insist on being here, now, in this body, and nowhere else, we are acting from our soul's understanding that we are always bigger than our problems.

The wild agitation diminishes, waves breaking against the imperturbable bulwark of the now. It always works. Not just when we are in the mood or when we are lucky. Always. In our darkest moments, in our greatest upsets, it always works.

Because it is true.

DEVELOPING THE PRACTICE

As we practice sitting in silence, the mind will more easily drop into the body. It becomes accustomed to following the breath. We begin to experience some stability when we sit. Distractions settle like sediments in a clear stream. When this happens, we can begin to investigate our mind and our emotions.

But first a note on the importance of our bodies. We might expect that the way of the mind leads us off into mental realms and away from everyday reality. Just the opposite is true. It brings our mind into our body for the first time. Mystical experience takes place in the body. We can transcend the limitations of our embodied existence only by fully embracing our embodiment. We felt this for ourselves when we took refuge in the present moment.

If we believe we must leave the body behind to have transcendent experience, we are running away from ourselves. We may have visions and fantasies, but nothing sensible will come of all our efforts. It is only in our bodies that we live, after all.

Unfortunately, a dominant strain of Western religious thought teaches that the body is vile and must be transcended. It is not the body that must be transcended but all ideologies, all instructions we were ever given on what to think, what to believe, what to be. These are the invisible chains we bind our freedom in. We will live in their constraint as long as we politely believe what we are told to believe and be who we are told to be.

Let us leave our social conditioning behind. Let us become really intimate with who we are when we put aside everything we are told to be. Let us trust ourselves. Let us find out.

Let us practice sitting still:

As you sit, let your mind follow your breath into silence. Let yourself feel your body. Feel the contact of your body with the chair or the floor. Feel the disposition of your legs and their sensations. Let yourself feel again your connection with the Earth.

Let your awareness move through your whole body, noticing any tension. When you find tension, let your awareness go to that tension and gently touch it. Letting the awareness touch the tension will often release it. If this does not happen, just touch the tension with awareness and move on for now, being aware of the whole body.

As you sit, you may feel pains in the body that you usually cover up with activity. Let your awareness go to them, one after another; touch them with awareness. Awareness is love. Touch the pain with the love that is your awareness. When you hold a pain in your awareness, even if you do nothing else to it, you may feel the pain diminish. Pain has a periodic structure like a wave, rising and falling. As we hold our pain in our awareness and experience its rising and falling nature, we become intimate with our pain.

Generally we run from pain and live in fear of it. Yet there is pain in our lives, and our lives are eased if the fear of pain is less. Sitting, attending to whatever pain is in our bodies, we can begin to know in an embodied way how pain arises and falls.

Sitting is not about encouraging pain. We earn no points for being macho and hurting our bodies. When we need to, we should move to lessen a pain. The trick is not to move too quickly: the unquiet mind will invent a thousand chimerical itches, tweaks, and pains to encourage us to move, and so unsettle our silence. Investigate the pain before moving. See what you can learn from it. It may have much to teach you. And then if you need to move, move.

The Mind and Its Thoughts

When we have followed the breath into the body and thus into silence, we can investigate the mind as we sit. Our everyday mind is distracted, running after whatever calls it, easily obsessed. This mind is often bored and restless. It sits in critical judgment of all we do. It is never satisfied, is always weighing and comparing. This mind resists being in the present moment. It runs after the past and toward the future. It is a narrow aperture through which we ordinarily see the world.

This is not the mind we are looking for. The ensouled mind knows pure awareness. It is nonjudgmental. It is patient. Because it sees the constantly unfolding miracle of our lives, it is never bored. Because it maintains its radiant awareness, it is never distracted. Because it sees clearly the relationship between the element and the whole, it does not judge. It always resides in the present moment because it knows that is where reality unfolds. For the mind that has let the soul come forward into it, there is no question about the meaning of life, for it knows the meaning directly.

THE ERROR OF NARCISSUS

Let us then work with the mind. In this practice, we study the nature of the everyday mind from the vantage of soul mind.

Sit comfortably and begin by following your breath. Allow your breath to entrain your mind, and allow your mind to relax.

When your mind has entered into silence, take time to enjoy it. Rest in it and become acquainted with it. This silence has no form or content, and yet it supports and nourishes you. In it all questions ultimately vanish without a trace, and we embody the answers. Let yourself be nourished by the silence.

Become aware of your awareness. You can easily take this awareness for granted, for it is always functioning perfectly. Who is aware of the silence? Pristine awareness in deep silence.

At some point that silence will be broken by a thought arising. Study the thought as it arises. To study the thought as it arises is to take the stance of the soul. Allow yourself to watch the thought, but do not move internally to the thought. Stay in the repose of silence, unmoving. As the thought arises, notice its look and feel, its form. Notice the contents of the thought. Do not interact with the contents of the thought, simply notice them.

Continue to watch the thought. As you do, you will see the life cycle of the thought. You simultaneously have the thought and study the thought. You will witness the birth, growth, reproduction, and death of the thought. Remarkably, in studying this one thought, you are studying the natural history of all the thoughts that have entered or ever will enter into consciousness.

What do we see when we observe the natural history of thought in human consciousness in real time in this way? The first thing we notice is that our minds are as fidgety as flies on a hot summer day. It is difficult to maintain the awareness that lets us observe thought. We begin to see our tendency to move toward a thought when it arises. We move toward the thought, give energy to it, and let it grow into a train of thoughts. We add associations and emotional accompaniment, and eventually abandon ourselves to it entirely. It does not matter whether the thought is great or small, high-minded or prurient. Our awareness collapses down from spaciousness to contraction. When we do this, we lose ourselves. We become no bigger than the thought, no wiser than the thought, no other than the thought. We spend most of our life lost in our mind. We forget we are the landscape and think that we are the passing play of light and shade that moves through it. Ephemeral images, not who we are.

To get lost in a thought even for a moment is to become Narcissus captivated by his image in the pool. Narcissus was a beautiful Greek youth, the favorite of Apollo. Golden, lithe, and distractible, he chanced upon a still pool one day as he was walking in the woods. He looked into the pool and beheld his reflection. This was before the age of mirrors. He was entranced. He had never seen anything so magical. Utterly enraptured, he sat by the pool all day. At night, he waited for the image to return, not sleeping, thinking of nothing else. When Apollo saw that there was no hope of prying Narcissus from his reflection in the pool, he took pity on him. He turned him into a flower, radiant again each spring.

The image in the pool was only a reflection of Narcissus. His mistake was not that he admired the ephemeral reflection. It would have been callous not to admire it. His mistake was to forget who he was. He identified himself completely with an image, and for this he lost his life. Every time we are lost in a thought, we repeat the error of Narcissus. For as long as we are lost in thought, we lose the present moment. For as long as we lose the present moment, we lose our life. For it is only in the present moment that we live.

We may be tempted to think that Narcissus entered some

special state. We may wonder whether it is not worth losing our life for such a deep encounter with beauty. Can our appreciation be as deep as his? What really happens when we remember all the time that we are the landscape and not the phenomena that pass through it? Was Narcissus the impassioned one, who merged with beauty? Does the practice of awareness put us on the sidelines, reduce us to voyeurs of our own experience, and stop us from really living? No. We are always lost, always gazing into the reflecting pool of our thoughts. The act of perceiving that our thoughts are just waves passing through us begins to wake us up. It gives us the chance to see that we have spent too long mesmerized by the pool and that we need to stand up and awaken to life.

Narcissus had the right instinct: to find ourselves we have to lose ourselves. His method, however, was shallow. When we study the natural history of thought in real time, we forget ourselves in the special sense that we progressively stop thinking of ourselves as "the person who thinks these thoughts." The very act of watching the thoughts begins to show us that we are more than this.

What could Narcissus have done to awaken rather than lose his life? Imagine him sitting at the pool, golden, enraptured. What could change the sad ending of this tale? Something very simple. While he gazes, he could ask himself the question: "Who is gazing at this image?" This question would have saved his life. It has the same power for us.

CROSSING OVER INTO SOUL MIND

Let us return to our study of thought as it arises in our awareness.

Follow your breath again into stillness. Let yourself again experience spacious, nonjudgmental, silent awareness. Reside in this awareness and wait until a

*thought arises. It may take time to return to silence, to
an awareness fine-grained enough to be able to watch a
thought arise.*

*Be gentle with yourself as you enter this awareness.
It is not important how often you get lost in thought.
What is important is how often you call yourself back.
When you call yourself back, let go of any judgment.
If you scold yourself for straying, you will only di-
minish your will to call yourself back. Be gentle when
calling yourself back. If we cannot be gentle with our-
selves in this way, how shall we ever be gentle?*

*So call yourself back gently. And repeatedly.
Just reside for a time in the still, spacious field of your
mind.*

Do not expect to have a single sitting in which all aspects
of thought arising into consciousness are played out for you
like a movie. Allow yourself the patience of the naturalist,
who is willing to stalk her quarry in all weathers and who
takes delight in glimpses. Over time, these moments accumulate into sustained observation, to the point where we can get
to know the quarry well.

*Sitting in silence, watch again as a thought arises.
Notice its qualities. Notice how it moves into your
awareness. Notice its first arising. As it enters your
awareness, how does it move? What are its form and
characteristics? Does it have an emotive quality? Do
not be attached to its characteristics, simply notice
them, as you would notice an animal you were stalking
for the first time. Let your thought be your quarry.
Stalk it.*

*Watch how it enters your consciousness. Where
does it come from? You may perceive an edge or border
to your field of awareness. You may experience the*

thought entering fully formed, crossing into your awareness from beyond this border.

You may experience your awareness as an ocean. You may experience the thought arising out of this ocean like a wave. Like a wave, it has a form. Like a wave, it has a structure and a periodicity. Be aware of these.

Then be aware of what happens to the thought when you refrain from interacting with it. You know what happens when we interact with a thought: we identify with and get lost in it. What happens if we reside in our pristine awareness and simply watch the thought, as we would watch a creature deep in a virgin wood?

The thought dwells for a time in our awareness. It then follows a natural arc of declining energy downward and returns to its source. We can actually see this happen. The wave falls back, returning to the ocean of awareness.

In letting a single thought return to the ocean, we have experienced something wondrous. By residing in our awareness and watching our thoughts, we have experienced that we are wider, broader, stabler than our thoughts. We have experienced that we are that in which the thoughts arise into awareness. In watching one thought return to its source, we have liberated that thought. In so doing we liberate ourselves: we see that we are not our thoughts. Until we experience it for ourselves, this fundamental truth is only another idea. Once we experience it, reality opens: we are infinitely vaster than any thought, than all thought. The limits of our thought are no longer the limits of our world.

We are not our thoughts. Seeing this, we have the beginnings of a radical change of perspective. In watching our thoughts, we adopt the perspective of the soul. Having adopted the soul's perspective once, we know the reality of soul mind in a visceral way. The view may be fleeting, the taste may be brief, but we can return to them until we have confirmed our experience in any way we need to. Having once seen the arising and falling nature of thought, we can always see it.

This gradual crossing over from everyday mind to soul mind is one of the epochal transitions of consciousness. When we identify with our thoughts, we have no idea who we really are. When we see them as waves passing through, we begin to find out.

We do not lose our everyday mind or our ability to get through day-to-day reality. Far from it. Soul mind contains everyday mind as one of its aptitudes, just as everyday mind contains instinct as one of its aptitudes. From the point of view of the soul, everyday mind is sacred, and ordinary life is the way.

Looking into Our Emotions

Resting stably in the present with our mind tuned to silence, we can become acutely aware of the way emotions arise in our awareness. This allows us to look deeply into the roots of a feeling that troubles us and to transform it.

EMOTION ARISING

In the silence of your sitting, watch as feelings arise.

Follow your breath into your body. Let your mind fall silent once again. The silent mind's awareness is very sharp. When emotion arises, experience what it feels like in the body. Notice where it is felt. Observe the way your body feels in that area. See whether it is tense or relaxed, and whatever other qualities it may have.

What does the emotion look like in the mind? What is its shape and form? What quality of energy does it bring as it enters your field of awareness? Just touch it with awareness. Do not feed it with energy. Do not turn your mind over to it. Do not let it swamp your awareness.

Note the arc of experience the emotion draws in your awareness. It arises and enters the field of your bodily and mental awareness. It dwells there for a time. Investigate what happens if you refrain from giving it energy, from attaching to it and elaborating on it. At a certain point, the emotion leaves your field of awareness. Like thoughts, emotions have periodic structures. They, too, are like waves. They rise, enter the field of awareness, and fall back. Arising and falling back is in the nature of waves and emotions.

When we test this, we begin to have a different relationship with our emotions. We begin to sense that if we are aware of what is going on in our mind and body, we can experience emotion as it arises. We realize that if we do not act on it, it falls back like waves. We begin to realize that we have tremendous freedom. Freedom to be aware of our emotions even as they arise. Freedom to work with them in real time. If we choose to give energy to an emotion and act upon it, we can do that. If we choose to let it pass, we can do that, and it will pass.

This understanding is contrary to how we usually experience emotions. Ordinarily, we are not aware of them as they arise. If a strong emotion, such as anger or desire, claims all our mind and energy, we become aware of it only after we have let ourselves be possessed by it.

Once we are possessed by an emotion, we cannot easily let it fall back like a wave. Instead, we find ourselves in the midst of a raging storm and know only that it is consuming us. Once this happens, the storm runs its course, with consequences we may regret. Our awareness is the landscape, the emotion the storm. As long as we reside in our awareness, the storm comes and goes and we are unchanged. It is when we forget ourselves, and lose touch with our awareness, that the storm engulfs us and may be damaging.

Watching the arising and falling of emotions is a profound practice. By letting a feeling fall back to its source without elaboration, we liberate it. By liberating a feeling, we liberate ourselves. We learn that we are not slaves to our emotions, except through inattention. Through simple training of our awareness, our inattention lessens, and we become more and more capable of exercising our choice. Do we let the feeling go? If we do, we must understand that this is not the same thing as repressing it. On the contrary, when we let the wave of feeling subside, it has moved through and gone, not been repressed.

There may be feelings, of course, that we do not want to let pass. If we have a loving impulse, we want to act on it. So we see it and act on it. There may be other feelings, long repressed, that we want to let in and work with. We will speak more about this in a little while. The important thing to note here is that there is all the difference in the world between anger we let in because we want to work with it consciously and anger that we let in blindly, which then possesses and uses us. The aim of this practice is to gain the spaciousness in which we know that we have a choice about what to do with every feeling as it arises. In this continual exercise of choice lies increasing freedom.

We are retraining the habits of a lifetime. We will often awaken to find ourselves possessed by some strong feeling. We must be patient. The important thing is how many times we awake and call ourselves back, not how many times we drift off.

WE ARE NOT OUR EMOTIONS

While sitting in silence, we can study another crucial aspect of who we are: the source of our feelings. Where do they come from? Investigate this as you sit, being aware of emotions while they arise. We identify closely with our emotions, perhaps even more closely than with our thoughts. And yet we are not our emotions. Our misidentification with our emotions is one of the primary blocks to a more expansive and accurate view of who we are.

Emotions may not even originate within our own physical and mental system. It helps to see emotions as waves of energy that enter us from outside. Emotions may come in from other people, from groups of people, and from impersonal sources. We may also have stored emotions that entered us in traumatic experiences, which we replay over and over when they are triggered.

It is powerfully liberating to consider feelings as forms of energy. Lust may arise in a form that surprises us with its strength. Violent impulses may arise that are out of character and have no basis we can place. A profound sadness may enter us. The sadness may seem unconnected to our experience; we may feel we are giving expression to a universal sadness. The emotions that arise in us in Washington, D.C., are very different from those that arise in Venice or in a virgin forest. This is not due to fantasy but at least in part to what is really going on there.

Where do our feelings come from? As you investigate this question remember that you are the landscape and not the storm. We need not feel guilty or ashamed about feelings that enter us. We are not responsible for every feeling that enters awareness. Feelings just enter. We are responsible only for what we *do* with them. It is up to us to choose what to do with each and every feeling. Do we let it go? Do we work with it? Do we let it take possession of us?

The same is true of thoughts. Thoughts and feelings are like guests. Although we are fully responsible for how we entertain them, we are not responsible for the fact that they showed up at the door. When we see this, we can begin to shed a great part of the burden of our guilt.

WORKING WITH PAINFUL FEELINGS

We all have a set of intuitions lying hidden just beneath painful feelings we do not want to probe. If we could only work through these feelings, the tremendous energy we bind up when we repress them could be ours, and the intuitions themselves could then emerge.

I would like to share a story from my own practice as an illustration. The painful feelings I needed to look into came from my concerns about the environment. During the years I worked as an environmental attorney, I struggled hard for what I considered positive change. And yet I found a fatalist quality in myself. The more I learned over the years as a specialist, the more depressing the picture of damage to the Earth's ecosystems became. I felt that we humans were doing irreparable and accelerating damage to the Earth. The rate of damage seemed to be inescapably increasing. Only a drastic change of course in the direction of our society seemed to have a chance of doing enough in time. But I was not sanguine about the possibility of change. What I knew of the inner workings of the legislative process, politics, and corporate behavior made it seem unlikely.

I feared for life on Earth. Fear can have a strong impact on the feeling tone of a psyche. It invites despair and hopelessness, a feeling of being defeated before we even start. I did not want to admit to myself that I had this fear at first. It seemed weak to feel it. And if I once admitted it, I saw no cure. Nevertheless, the fear was there. You cannot spend very long on a cushion facing a wall, as I was doing, without getting to know your preoccupations, your obsessions, your fears. I decided to spend a full week's intensive meditation retreat looking into this fear, to see what I could learn of it.

I spent the first couple of days preparing the field. I let myself sink into practicing the way of the mind. I rose before dawn and meditated into the night. I felt the mind and heart clear. I then invited any thoughts or feelings about the fate of the Earth that might wish to come forward. I watched thoughts and feelings as they arose. I watched to see which ones repeated themselves, which ones carried the strongest charge. It was a field trip into a part of my inscape that I had never consciously entered before. Though this fear had exerted a strong influence on my conscious life, I had never looked into it awake. I determined that I would not stop until I could walk this part of my inscape comfortably.

I discovered a belief I held tacitly but firmly: that human beings would destroy all life on Earth. This belief was so deeply troubling that I had averted my gaze from it. I had never admitted to myself that I held the belief. Rather than naming this belief and looking into it, I had ceded it tremendous power over my feelings.

I decided to examine this belief with a thought experiment. I allowed myself to think of the most likely scenarios by which humans could destroy the biosphere. The scenarios included ecocatastrophe and global nuclear war. But this was not just an experiment in thought. I needed to engage my feelings too. So I allowed myself to feel global nuclear war. I imagined the devastation from the war itself and the nuclear winter that would follow. The destruction of people and of other living things. Of all culture. Of everything I loved. These thoughts had been too charged to think before. There was too much fear around them. The fear prevented me from looking into them, froze me into numb ignorance.

Unless we admit and accept the possible loss of what we love and fight for, how can we act freely? It is like our own life. Until we accept our death, how can we accept our life? If we spend our life denying death, how much of our life will we ever see? If we do not look into the loss of what we love, its transience, how can we truly appreciate it? How much of it will we have even seen?

I felt the destruction of life on Earth through the whole of a very long day. And then what I knew about Gaia started to enter my thoughts. It happened spontaneously when I had let the viscous matter of my fear run clear. Gaia emerged into my awareness on her own, and I began to develop a more visceral feeling for Gaia. In the Gaian view, all natural systems are interconnected into a single living superorganism, the biosphere itself, which maintains comfortable conditions on Earth for all of life.

I thought about the life story of Gaia. Gaia has been alive from the time the earliest bacteria swarmed over the face of the whole planet. That was, by current estimates, almost three and a half billion years ago. As a form of life, Gaia has survived the impacts of meteors and other natural catastrophes that have several times destroyed most living species then extant. The dinosaurs died; Gaia lived. Each time there was a great dying, new species emerged and life continued to evolve. If the dinosaurs had not died off, our mammalian ancestors would never have had a chance to flourish. As I saw into the pertinacity of Gaia, it became clear that no matter how humans acted, Gaia would go on living. It seemed possible that we might destroy human life. It seemed likely that we would extirpate a significant percentage of species now living, whether or not we killed off our own species. As I meditated through these scenarios, though, it came to me as an unshakable conviction that Gaia would go on.

It then returned to my memory that the Sun is impermanent. When it reaches the end of its life cycle, it will explode in a stellar nova. Then will life go out of Gaia at last. Until then, Gaia, who is only middle-aged, will live on, no matter what mistakes we human beings make.

This was deeply comforting. I started to identify more with Gaia and less with this small body. We are, I began to see, a luminous, conscious part of Gaia. When I saw this, the fear dissolved. And with it what had been for me a heavy burden: I had felt that it was up to me as an environmental activist to change human behavior. To save the Earth. I knew the size of the problem and how few people were working for change. Looking back on it, I see the arrogance of my assumption of this burden. It was never mine to pick up. The burden was nevertheless lifted when I looked into my fear that week.

When we look into a painful repressed feeling, we are healing a wound with the touch of our awareness. Awareness is no other than love. It is characteristic of this practice that when we move into a wound and heal it, other unseen wounds are simultaneously healed. There is a profound and startling economy in the soul.

Deep Listening

Listening is an aspect of awareness. In the way of the mind we can use listening—deep listening—as a tool of transformation. We can hear our way into the wisdom encoded in Nature; we can thereby learn to hear, perhaps for the first time, what other people are telling us. During one retreat, birds and insects taught me how to listen and to hear.

It was at one of our intensive seven-day retreats at a mountain retreat center, then run by the Los Angeles Zen Center, where I lived and studied while working at environmental law. During the retreat, we woke at 3:45 in the morning and, with various breaks, meditated in silence until 9:00 at night.

The retreat center faces west near the top of Apple Canyon, nestled into the inland ridge of mountains running down along the Southern California coast. Three hours' drive east of Los Angeles, the center is a mile up. If you walk a few hundred feet higher, to the top of the ridge, you look down on Palm Springs, in the desert a mile below. This easternmost ridge of coastal mountains catches whatever moisture remains in the air moving east on the prevailing wind from the Pacific Ocean. It comes down as summer thunderstorms and winter snow, leaving the desert, inland and below, in the mountains' rainshadow. This precipitation makes the canyon moist for that part of the world. Ancient cedars and pines mix in the canyon with younger pine and scrub oak. Some of the ancient trees seem as big as well-watered middle-aged redwoods. Spotted owls, cougar, and rattlesnakes are seen. A profusion of ferns and wildflowers grow in the meadows. Groups of acorn woodpeckers fly around together flashing black and white and red, their calls loud, raucous laughs.

As the retreat began, a story I have always liked came to me. It is about Avalokiteshvara, the archetype of compassion. In the story, Avalokiteshvara is about to leave this world and enter a blissful state for all time. He has worked hard while on Earth and is looking forward to being reunited with the source of his being. Nothing could make him happier. Just as he is about to cross the threshold between worlds, however, someone kills a rabbit and it screams. Avalokiteshvara stops and lets the scream pierce his heart. He decides in that instant that he will not enter Nirvana while any living being suffers on the Earth. He will voluntarily return to the Earth to help all beings.

I was moved by this story and intrigued by the role that listening played in it. I wanted to develop compassion but did not know how. I wanted to be able once again to hear the natural world speak but did not know the way. The story implied that if we just listen with our whole being, and let ourselves be penetrated by what we hear, compassion will come automatically.

For that seven-day period, I decided I would devote myself entirely to listening to what was around me, not thinking about what I heard. Not judging it or drawing conclusions, but just listening. Deep listening. I walked to the first meditation of the retreat admiring the stars. They were clear in the middle of the mountain night, from my vantage of a mile high. A shooting star flared brief and white in the cloudless sky, and I longed that my own life be such a brilliant flashing forth.

We meditated in a temporary building of plywood with

open screen windows. This made it easy to hear everything that was going on around us in the natural world. Apple Canyon is a fairly narrow canyon. Surmounted by peaks, with its ancient pines and cedar, it is an acoustically clear space. The silence in the mountain night was velvety and soft. After an hour or so of meditation, still well before dawn, a great horned owl called. It was signing off after a night of hunting in its deep and breathy voice. The owl's voice is a nighttime voice, dark and soft around the edges. The owl flies in almost perfect silence, and one hears it only when it wants to be heard. Dawn came, and brightness grew. Then, and only gradually, other species of birds began to call in morning's first light and warmth.

As the week went on, the acuity of my listening increased. I began to distinguish clearly the songs of individual species of birds. I could not put a face to the calls of all of them, but as I began to recognize the calls, I sensed a pattern in their sequence and timing that I had not before perceived.

The more I listened the more I began to listen like a bird. I began to hear an ecology of sound in the canyon that I had never imagined. I began to hear that each species had a time in the early morning to make its call undisturbed by others. Each would briefly claim the whole of Apple Canyon for itself. Each species had several long minutes of clear airtime. The entire valley would be filled with the sound of its song alone. There would follow a silence, and the next species would begin its call. "Here I am! Another day! I am here to defend a territory, find a mate, gorge on insects, on berries, feed my young, live my life to the hilt!" Each species would have the soundscape to itself until the round of calls was complete. Then an overlap of calls would come, as morning light diffused into the canyon. When the full Sun crested the enclosing peaks, and its light poured like fire into the valley, the August heat would boom forward, almost audible.

It was time for the insects. While the birds, being warm-blooded, woke early, the cold-blooded insects waited for the Sun's warmth to begin their songs. Then the crickets and the cicadas, beetles and flies would add to the music. It was the deep, loud pulse of the crickets that acted like a continuo and bound all the music of the birds and insects into a symphony of sound.

This was a performance that rewarded deep listening, day after day. I began to notice that I could follow several sounds attentively at the same time. I had assumed that I could hold only one sound in focus at a time, to which any other sounds provided an aural backdrop. This turned out to be a misconception. I could listen to seven or eight sounds simultaneously. I gained a deeper appreciation of Mozart, who could listen individually to all the instruments in a symphony as they played together.

There are many ways to really listen. Each of them opens the heart. One that came on its own, as these things do, was a way to listen to small birds. Titmice and chickadees would perch near where I sat meditating. They would sing solo arias. I would breathe with the birds' songs, letting the songs register in this body too. As they came to visit and sing, one after the other, I let myself feel the birds' breath, their heartbeat. Two bodies, one song.

This practice of deep listening occupied me fully for the seven days of the retreat, during which time I was careful not to talk. When the retreat ended, there was a picnic lunch. A friend came up to me and started talking. A startling experience followed.

But here I have to back up for a moment. For some years before the retreat, I was aware that the way I listened to other people was not what I wanted it to be. Though people regarded me as a good listener, I did not feel that I was. I felt unable to give the person who was speaking to me my undivided attention. While listening, I was working on my response. The tenor of the response was dictated by how I perceived my encounter with the other person. I might wish to impress, amuse, seduce, or instruct. Depending on what I was seeking to achieve, the response would be composed while the other person spoke. Not just composed in a rough sort of way, but on a screen that floated before my eyes as if in the air, as though I had a conversational version of the TelePrompTer that politicians use and that allows them to read a speech while their audience sees only a piece of clear glass. So much energy went into composing my answers that they would be posted on the screen in time for me to edit them before I read them off.

I was terribly tired of this way of speaking with others but had no real idea of how to go beyond it and become more spontaneous. The answer came at that picnic. When my friend spoke, I found myself staring into his eyes and just listening, as I had listened to the birds the entire week. Just listening. No thoughts of my own, just hearing the thoughts of my friend. There was a moment of panic. I thought, "He's going to stop speaking any second now, and I've prepared nothing! I will have nothing ready to say!"

I let the panic go. I decided to see what would happen if I gave no thought at all to a response and just kept listening to my friend. As it happened, when he stopped speaking, I started speaking. I had no idea of what I would say, but I said something he accepted well enough.

From deep listening had come spontaneity, and it has stayed that way ever since. The TelePrompTer vanished, and it feels like being on vacation in my own life. Nature's lessons, taken in, are long-lived ones.

The Last Thought

Let us move into the ultimate question posed by thought. It lies at the heart of the way of the mind and is the strait gate to the soul's perspective.

The question is this: "Who am I?"

We have all faced this question at some time. How have we answered it? I was discouraged for about twenty-five years because I did not believe it was possible to find a real answer. Using the approach of analytic philosophy, I tried convincing myself that the question itself was nonsense. But this approach does not satisfy our need to make sense of our lives.

Let us see how the way of the mind can help us here.

Take a moment to survey whatever tools of analytic thought you have honed throughout your life. Perhaps you learned them in psychology, business, science, literary criticism, public relations, or law. Perhaps you are skeptical of all claims put before you and enjoy teasing out their defects. Maybe you feel that you have a systematic approach—say, deconstructionism or critical thinking—that you can rely on in every situation. You feel you can use it to see through false claims, to avoid being taken in. So much the better!

If you are a skilled practitioner of analytic thought, this

stage on the way of the mind is where you can put all your skills in play to their ultimate advantage. How so? Because in this practice we want to believe nothing, accept nothing, rely on nothing, until we have exhausted our analytic capacity in testing it. What happens when we turn our skepticism on our skepticism? Our cynicism on our cynicism? Our deconstructionism and critical thinking on themselves? What happens when we turn all our ability to see through things back on ourselves? What do we see? Who am I?

DOING THE WORK

How do we investigate this question: "Who am I?" It requires the stability that comes from sitting in silence. It requires patience. It is an ultimate question, and we cannot hurry the birth of a true answer. When I began to practice, this question was my sole practice for three years, and I have been working with it in one way or another ever since. I do not ever expect to put the question to rest.

When we do this investigation we are not learning something, as we learn chemistry or cooking. We are not acquiring anything. Nor are we giving anything up, though we may give up notions along the way that no longer ring true. Instead, we are preparing in an unseen way for a fundamental shift in perspective toward our thoughts, feelings, body, experience. We cannot effect the shift directly, much as we might like to. But if we work in absolute sincerity with the tools we have at hand, the shift will take care of itself.

Although the practice begins and is rooted in silence, once you take it up, you will find all of life reflected in it, and you will find it reflected within every smallest gesture that you make. Now onto the thin ice. Let us examine some of the areas of inquiry that our question will bring us into.

THOUGHTS AND FEELINGS:

Follow your breath into the stillness of your body. Let your mind go silent and ask yourself:

> *Am I my thoughts and feelings, or my memories of them, or any combination of them?*
>
> *Even if I am not my individual thoughts and feelings considered alone or in any set or arrangement, am I nevertheless my neurotic patterns? My childhood traumas? My righteous and self-righteous anger? My most secret inward shame I would never tell anyone?*
>
> *Am I all my sophistication, so carefully contrived? My poems, my memories, my original thinking, my kindest thoughts? Who am I when thought and feeling are completely put aside?*

OPINIONS:

Follow your breath into the stillness of your body. Let your mind go silent and ask yourself:

> *Am I my views of things, my considered opinions, my ideology, my nationality?*
>
> *I may have a political ideology that I consider central to the improvement of human life, whether conservative or liberal. I may hold religious views that I believe are true and unquestionable. I may believe I know what is right and what is wrong. I may believe that some core part of me is American or French or South African or whatever my nationality is.*
>
> *Am I any of these opinions or any set or arrangement of them?*

SOCIAL ROLES:

Follow your breath into the stillness of your body. Let your mind go silent and ask yourself:

> *Am I the roles I play throughout my life?*
> *I play a variety of social roles, and I identify with them. I may be a spouse and a parent. Are these who I am? I may be a doctor or a dancer, a minister or a madam. Are these who I am?*
> *Our culture invests billions of dollars every year in teaching us through ads that we are, in our deepest essence, consumers of material goods. Are the ads right?*
> *Who am I when I put every social role aside?*

BODY:

Follow your breath into the stillness of your body. Let your mind go silent and ask yourself:

> *Am I this body that will die one day?*
> *We are getting to know the body better through practice. It feels different, seems to have an entrée to wisdom we have never seen before.*
> *Am I the body? Even if I feel an expanded sense of body, even if it extends to the whole Earth, am I that body?*

SEXUALITY AND GENES:

Follow your breath into the stillness of your body. Let your mind go silent and ask yourself:

*Am I just a self-replicating animal, hoping and strug-
gling to be something more?*

*Sexuality is a central feature of my experience. Am
I fooling myself by searching for a meaning in my life?
Am I nothing but a machine for passing on my genes?*

Is all the rest an illusion?

THE SENSE OF SELF:

Follow your breath into the stillness of your body. Let your
mind go silent and ask yourself:

Am I this "I" that is at the center of all my experience?

*This sense of "I" is my most familiar companion
since my first memory. It is where I lodge my sense of
self. It feels real, as though there is an "I" present in all
my experience. The contents of experience come and
go, but they seem real and make sense only with refer-
ence to an unchanging "I."*

Am I this self?

Who am I if I am not this self?

THE NATURE OF THOUGHT AND CULTURE:

Follow your breath into the stillness of your body. Let your
mind go silent and ask yourself:

*Can I have experience independent of my culture and
beyond all thought?*

*Imagine thought itself as an organism that seeks to
live on our awareness. See thought as bacteria growing
in a lab dish, where our awareness is the food that
thought feeds on.*

Notice that thought seeks to perpetuate itself by

continuously making more of itself. See thought repro-
ducing in your awareness, occupying the field of your
awareness. Thought reproduces culture, analysis, fan-
tasy, and all other forms of itself simply to occupy the
space of your awareness.

As thought fills your awareness, what is left forever
untouched by it?

The primary evolutionary strategy used by thought is to com-
plicate our search for who we are so thoroughly, with ever
more refined forms of itself, that we never see beyond it, and
so never notice that thought itself is a predator on our energy,
time, and awareness.

When we are completely still, thought is left behind. We
know things directly. Duality, thought's handmaiden, van-
ishes with it. Our perception is pellucid, our knowledge of
who we are so fills us that the question falls away.

No "now" remains, because we are only in the now. No
yesterday, no tomorrow, no today.

When we enter this field of direct knowing, we are
refreshed by its purity and its contentment. Though it
extends throughout the Universe, it rejoices in a snail and in
the snail's trail of slime. It shrinks from nothing, judges nothing, needs nothing. Elation and depression are specks of dust
floating in its immensity and do not cling to it. It grasps nothing and is itself ungraspable. Residing in it, the ruckus of
thought is remote, like waves against a distant shore.

When we are coextensive with this natural perception of
ourselves, a moment will come when we begin to move out of
this state into our normal mind. The radiance dissipates; twi-
light comes to Eden. This is a very valuable moment. In this
crucial transition, we can clearly witness the killing acquisi-
tiveness of thought. We were just receiving and perceiving,
directly and before thought. And then, within a picosecond,
thought enters. It acquires our perception for itself by casting

its flexible net. Our perception is caught and dies to its spontaneity in the catching. In this very moment, we are exiled
from Eden into the dusty corridors of thought, which spreads
all our perceptions like butterflies pinned upon spreading
boards. Later, the perceptions are categorized, taxonomized,
stored, fumigated. Who am I then?

Our normal waking mind is in its own way fast asleep.
Lulled by thought, it bears the same relationship to soul mind
that our sleeping dreaming mind bears to it. Who am I when
not lulled by thought? When I am the master, not the servant,
of thought? Who am I beyond all thought and feeling?

LIVING WITH THE QUESTION

We need to apply radical doubt to every aspect of our mental
constructs. As we do this, we experience a forgetting and a
remembering.

The more mental constructs we have and the more carefully they are elaborated, the more time and effort it takes. If
we have wholly identified with thought, and cultivated it in
well-kept gardens of abstruse design, treasuring our recondite
imaginings as we walk through mental landscapes where few
can follow, then we have a lot of work to do. At the same
time, the more we have constrained ourselves to the limits of
thought, the more we will enjoy being unbound.

What is the forgetting that this practice brings about? We
gradually forget to put on our shackles when we wake up in
the morning. We let go of the notion that what I am in my
essential nature is an "I," a person with a certain description,
certain prejudices, certain roles. We begin to forget our
drama. Or if not to forget it, to take it less seriously. Like
everyone, we will have put a large proportion of our energy
into our drama. We will have taken slights and turned them
into the Trojan War; we will have had mystical visions and

thought them terribly important; we will have seen into social problems and declared the world is ending; we will have fallen in love and claimed that no human being has ever loved so much; we will have never stopped complaining and gossiping and self-justifying even for a moment. In short, we will have been the impresario of our own melodrama. We will have done such a convincing job that we, too, were taken in and thoroughly believed the drama ourselves.

As we ask "Who am I?" with absolute sincerity, we begin to take our drama a little less seriously. We continue for a long time to spin it out. But we are apt to catch ourselves at it and laugh at ourselves for it. It is a wonderful way to have a laugh. Who is the joke on?

As we apply radical skepticism to every construction in our inner landscape, we might expect ourselves to get more and more cynical. Happily, just the opposite is the case. As we let the question "Who am I?" eat through every social role, every notion of ourselves, we get not more but less cynical. The practice is an acid that dissolves cynicism itself.

Cynicism is a defeated stance, whereas asking our question is a strongly positive one. To ask it is to take the chance that life has meaning and that I am as well equipped as any human being ever born to find out that meaning for myself. Why should I listen to anyone else anymore? To my own cynicism? Who am I?

Why not take this chance? Conventional forms of thought will, in a sensitive and perceptive mind, almost certainly lead to cynicism, in the circumstances of the world as we find them. Why not question the conventional forms of thought, including all currently chic intellectual approaches to reality? Why not be completely radical in thought? It leads to a comfort beyond cynicism, a peace beyond hope.

If alienation is what we forget, what do we remember as we do the practice? We gradually remember the soul's perspective. We remember the ungraspable movement of being that we always are. We begin to know ourselves as that movement, as a vast blue sky through which a few clouds occasionally pass, and as the body that made the Universe.

As we remember, we become more ordinary, less grandiose, less given to highs and lows, more equable, less obsessed with being special, more willing to let every experience pass, knowing that experience is transitory and trusting that whatever comes next will be all right.

We stop thinking we have to run from our body, from our abilities, from our successes and failures. We begin to accept everything about ourselves. We become less pretentious. We start meeting people and not thinking about what they look like. We accept our limitations. Instead of pretending we have no anger, we admit we are irascible and work on it.

We let ourselves admit that we have a museumful of foibles, like everyone else. We begin to let ourselves be ordinary. We begin to like ourselves. And to appreciate the miracle of every moment. Each ordinary moment. Just this. Just now. Clear and real. Nothing else needed. Nothing else at all.

So let the question penetrate your every thought, every action throughout the day.

As you wake in the morning, ask "Who is waking?" As you wash your face, "Who is washing?" As you eat breakfast, "Who is eating?" As you go to the office, "Who is commuting?"

Ask the question with curiosity. It need not be a harsh question. You can ask it like a lover.

As you answer the phone, "Who is answering?" As you sit in a meeting, "Who is sitting here?" As you eat lunch, ask it. As you use the toilet, ask it.

While you have a conversation, ask it. As you

awake from a daydream, ask it. As you find yourself in a sex fantasy, ask it. As you make love, ask it. As you get drunk, ask it. When you are angry, ask it. When you are gleeful, ask it.

Ask it when you are lonely. When you are depressed. When you are doing the dishes and sweeping the floor. While you are having an argument, while you are paying the bills. While you are pulling weeds. As you fall asleep. When you cannot fall asleep.

Let the question go into your breath and fill your body. Let it sink into your bones and blood and there produce the answer you are looking for. Deep, deep within the body.

Let yourself feel that you will ask it until you know for sure. Let yourself feel that no one ever born was better equipped to answer it than you.

Let yourself know that it is only a matter of asking with absolute sincerity and thoroughgoing pertinacity. Let yourself know that being stubborn finally has its use.

Let yourself know that you will never stop until you drive yourself sane.

Begin to know yourself intimately.

Less Stress,
More Creative Intuition

Pursuing the way of the mind, at whatever level we do so, reduces our load of stress and allows us greater access to our intuition. Some stress is unavoidable. If we find ourselves standing next to a jackhammer while it is operating, we will take in stress. If our partner is depressed or ill, we will be affected. Although we take stress in, we need not hold on to it. We shed stress by touching it with awareness.

As we become familiar with following the breath into the body, we become able to do it throughout the day, whatever circumstances we are in. The more we do this, the more sensitive we become to the condition of our body in each moment. If we are in the body and a stressful experience happens, we will feel the stress enter our awareness. We will feel how the body tenses, clenches, holds on to the stress. We may tense our stomach or shoulders. We may constrict our diaphragm. Each of us has a variety of ways to react physically to stressful experiences. As we enter into the experience of the body we become aware of them, and so we can release them.

Often, simply focusing our attention on the tension will release it. When the body tenses, it would like to relax soon thereafter. When we bring our awareness to the tension—say, to our clenched stomach—it will often relax spontaneously, tension flowing out like a wave. If it does not, we can stretch, take a walk, work out, have a massage. We can experiment until we find what works. The ability to be acutely aware of our body allows us to shed stress as we take it in, rather than letting it build to levels that can be damaging. Life is stressful. We can enjoy it much more if we know how to shed the stress as it comes in.

There is another kind of stress that is avoidable, but it is much subtler and more difficult to become aware of. This is the whole realm of stress we cause ourselves because of the way we have formed our inner landscape. We have all built ourselves a strong fortification of ideas and feelings. We stake out certain territories of thought, opinion, loyalty, and feeling as ours. We identify with them. We are them. We will defend them against all comers. Our mind is our castle. When this happens, we are always on the alert for intruders. Every idea, every opinion, every fact, every experience, every ambition that does not agree with ours is felt as potentially hostile, potentially a threat.

The most perfect illustration of the way we build and defend fortifications in the inscape comes from Kafka. In his surreal, luminous story "The Burrow," we see the world from the point of view of a mole. We experience his world as he builds his burrow and fortifies its central hiding place, a room he calls his castle keep. The mole never stops laboring at his defenses. He is always feverish and always fearful. He may run out of prey; he may be eaten at any moment by an unsuspected predator. To the degree that we identify with our constructions of thought and feeling, we are Kafka's mole.

The more we follow the way of the mind, the more we will gain the inner poise from which we know that we are not our thoughts and feelings. We gain the courage to leave our burrow, to walk out of our castle keep, and so to explore parts of our inner landscape we never knew were there.

We quit one castle keep, stroll about our inner landscape

for a while, and then we build another. The new one will be more commodiously built and less in need of defense. Each time we quit one, build and then take up residence in another, we do it knowing it is a temporary residence. This offers a lighter way of living than we ever had before.

No more do we have to rise to the bait each time and enter every argument. No more do we waste our energy worrying about the perfection of our fortifications. Instead, we may choose to watch from our ramparts and enjoy the show. Once we take up this lighter view, each of our castles becomes just a resting place on the way to ever more spacious lodgings.

The less stress we make for ourselves, the more we have access to our creative intuition. What we think of as creative intuition is the soul's ability to tap into the inner structure of being, which we share with all there is, and open it to us as we seek to solve some problem. While we are primarily engaged in building inner castles and defending them from imaginary foes, we are not very able to hear the voice of intuition. Its voice is a still small voice, and we have to be clear and quiet to hear it.

We may be surprised that the way of the mind leads to creative intuition. The method of the way may seem cold and impersonal, the antithesis of creative intuition. If we think this, we have more to learn about both the way of the mind and creative intuition. Remember that genuine attention, open attention, curious attention, patient attention is nothing other than love. It is this attention we bring to bear on ourselves. This method is pure love, reflected in the entityless eye of pure awareness. Its aim is for us to awaken from illusion and enjoy life intimately and well.

As we follow this way, we see that we hold a great many mistaken ideas about the creative intuition. A romantic myth about it says there is a capricious muse we need to woo. She comes or goes, we know not where or why. We must be willing to have unproductive days, sleepless nights, personal dramas, destructive habits, depressions. These are the tokens we offer her in this treacherous courtship.

Nothing could be further from the truth. The creative intuition is not a capricious will-o'-the-wisp. It is not demanding, damaging, and all the rest, but is always available and absolutely reliable. It is as impersonal, as ever sustaining, as our awareness itself. And the better shape we are in psychically the more access we have.

We need engage in no uncertain courtship. We need only know how to open, which is done by getting out of the way, by following the way of the mind: be still; be silent; be filled.

When we clutch our suffering, our ideas, our victimhood, our need for success, our insistence on our brilliance, we create a barrier impervious to the creative intuition's flow. Creativity is our normal state of being. In following this way we simply return to what and who we are. The result is boundless access to the creative flow again at last.

The Eureka Principle

Here is a simple secret: a way out is always looking for a way in.

In the ordinary situations in which we need solutions, this principle is easy to apply: a creative solution is always open to the right invitation. We begin by focusing on the problem. We then follow the breath into our body and sit in inner silence, waiting, open, until the answer arises naturally in our mind. For matters of day-to-day concern, it seldom takes long.

We also face larger tasks. Our life or career may turn on solving a problem remote from the normal run of things. Can we find a systematic and reliable way to apply this Eureka Principle to such questions? First, let us look at three examples in which people used stillness to find breakthrough solutions that no one else had seen. The examples come from Mohandas Gandhi's political work, Barbara McClintock's work on genetics, and my own work as an environmental lawyer.

Mohandas Gandhi's middle years were given to working for Indian independence, which was not work that gave onto easy solutions. During the years 1914 to 1919, Gandhi developed the principles of his Satyagraha, or nonviolent resistance. He organized campaigns and had some early successes. But there were also failures, disarray within the independence movement, and a lack of clarity within Gandhi himself. By 1927, the independence movement, though full of energy, was without direction. No single event had yet catalyzed the nation into a unified vision or coordinated action.

By the winter of 1929–1930, the tension was at a breaking point. Gandhi had emerged as the central figure in the movement. There was a national meeting of the Indian congress—the political coalition opposed to British rule—that agreed to follow Gandhi's lead and use a nonviolent approach. But the congress also demanded action. Gandhi was told to devise a plan for nonviolent revolutionary action. It was clear that if he could not do so quickly, the moment for nonviolence would be lost and violence would break out. When one studies the life of Gandhi, this is a clear turning point. The energy had built up like water behind a dam. He had to channel it or it would burst. What was his plan?

He had no idea, but he did have a method. He went into retreat in a hut on his ashram. He decided he would wait for the still small voice of his intuition to tell him what to do. Meantime, he would meditate and pray, while the entire nation waited—and watched, expecting brilliance but living with a short fuse.

From contemporaneous stories we have of people he spoke with, including the poet Rabindranath Tagore, it is clear that Gandhi was not playing a part. He was not pretending to be in retreat in order to dramatize his own importance. He really did not know what to do, but he knew that if he waited with openness and sincerity a solution would come. He was prepared to wait as long as necessary. It took six weeks of quiet sitting, meditation, praying, thinking. No phones, no press conferences. Just the empty space of his hut on the ashram. Imagine having that trust in your practice.

Imagine a major American or European political figure going into retreat during a political crisis while the whole nation watched and waited.

And then, one day, Gandhi emerged and said he would walk to the sea and make salt. The British officials thought he had lost his mind and become a harmless eccentric. But he knew what he was doing. As he walked several hundred miles to the sea, from village to village, thousands joined him. In an era before media events, this was a media event. When he got to the sea, he scooped up a basin of seawater, and when it dried, salt was left. Why had Gandhi decided to make salt? Because making salt was a British monopoly. All Indians were prohibited by law from making salt. And yet every Indian used salt every day for all the humblest things in life. The salt laws touched every Indian of all castes. By making salt Gandhi was nonviolently claiming the right to live life as an Indian beyond the reach of British interference.

The country went wild. It was the galvanic moment that was needed. The move to independence by nonviolent means became unstoppable.

Barbara McClintock, who died in New York in 1992, was one of the great scientists of the century. She became interested in plants and in her own consciousness early on. She was to combine the two interests in a way that led to a breakthrough in genetics and an eventual Nobel Prize.

As a young woman, McClintock wanted to study the nature of genes. In those early days, one studied genes by studying Indian corn, or maize. Genes could not be studied directly. No one had ever seen them. All you could do was study the inherited characteristics in corn plants. To do this you had to count corn kernels. You would study the different colors and shapes and sizes of the kernels in an ear of corn.

You planted the corn the next year and carefully bred the plants. You then studied the kernels this time around, kept track of them all, and so on. Endless ears of corn, years of work, infinite patience.

McClintock loved her plants. Over the course of a season, she would get to know every single one of the hundreds of plants in her experimental plot. She would know it as an individual. She would know its parents. She would visit it as it was growing and get to know its look, its feel, its personality. She would develop, as she said, "a feeling for the organism." She gained this degree of intimacy with all the hundreds of her corn plants, every year all over again. To us they would all look like corn plants. To her they were as different as our closest friends seem to us.

Perhaps it is not hard to be a genius. Maybe all it takes is tremendous focus. Newton said that he solved problems that others did not because he would stay focused on them until the solution came. McClintock had this focus too.

By simply studying the ears of corn through generation after generation, geneticists had worked out a great deal about how genes functioned. There were also, of course, many unanswered questions. McClintock became interested in a difficult one. It involved the transmission of a trait that seemed to disobey all the laws that corn geneticists had worked out. The trait moved around inexplicably. It seemed an enigma that was impossible to solve with the tools at hand.

Remember that at this time no one had ever seen genes. They were only the abstract contours of a theory. Everything that was known about genes was known by studying the impacts of their action on the shape and color of corn kernels. It was like trying to draw a complete psychological portrait of someone using only a record of the telephone numbers that person dialed.

Yet McClintock continued to study her corn and all the

cases of the transmission of the moving trait. She accumulated vast quantities of data on cards, recording it, studying it, looking for patterns to emerge from it that might make a discernible shape. Bits of ideas came, and partial results, but the enigma remained. It was not possible that a trait could move around like the one she was studying. Genes were supposed to be reliable replicators!

McClintock had always been interested in consciousness as well. When she was a girl she loved to run, jumping high up as she ran along. After a while, she would come into a clarity that she enjoyed. She was later delighted to find that a similar practice was used by some Tibetan lamas. Over the years of familiarizing herself with the corn, she had let herself use this clarity of consciousness to do something no other geneticist had done. She let herself "think like corn." She would let herself merge with the object of her study, her contemplation, her love. This is the technique of the mystic, as well as of the greatest scientists.

One day, when all of the work was fresh in her mind, she was walking. She sat down and let herself think like corn. Using her intuitive mind as a microscope, McClintock let herself sink deep into a place where she could become one of the genes. She began to see things from the perspective of a gene. She let herself absorb their reality. She suddenly got a series of intuitions about how these genes worked, how they moved, and why they did what they did. The genes did not conform to prior theory. Instead of moving predictably, they sometimes jumped around. She saw how it happened and why. It made sense of all the data, even as it destroyed a lot of theory.

McClintock came up out of being a gene, returned to her normal awareness, and went back to the lab. She checked the data against her vision. The vision explained the facts. Theory would have to change.

It did. She wrote up a version of her vision in the grammar

of genetic theory. Her discovery is now known as jumping genes. Though it took a long time to be accepted, it is standard and central in genetic theory today. Her method, however, had carried her well ahead of her colleagues. She knew enough not to mention that she had merged her consciousness with the genes to find her result. In her time, scientists would have been unprepared to accept her mystical method. It took many years for her work to be fully understood and accepted. With the Nobel Prize came a recognition of her originality. How many scientists today have the fluidity of perception to follow McClintock's method and merge with the object of their study?

In 1990, I founded the Los Angeles office of the Natural Resources Defense Council (NRDC). Despite all the environmental problems of Southern California, none of the national environmental groups had an office of lawyers and scientists in Los Angeles. After a couple of years of talking to people and raising the funds from the Los Angeles community, we had an office going. It was working on air and water, transportation, lead exposure for inner-city children, and a range of other things, all of them enormous issues for a small staff.

One of the issues I wanted to tackle but could not find a purchase on was development along the remaining natural coastline from Los Angeles south to the Mexican border. Most of the undeveloped land not owned by the military was owned by huge land-development companies. After all, it was some of the most valuable land in America. I did not see a way to take on the most powerful developers in the country. Besides, I was busy.

The impetus to do something came at a lunch in Pasadena at the California Institute of Technology—CalTech. One of my tasks as head of the Los Angeles office of the NRDC was to meet with people who were interested in the work we did,

particularly those who could help support it. So I had lunch
at CalTech with Murray Gell-Mann, a physicist who had won
a Nobel Prize for his work on subatomic particles. He also sat
on the board of the MacArthur Foundation, one of the
wealthiest American foundations. Both he and the foundation
had strong environmental interests.

We met at the faculty club, a genteel Southern California
Spanish building. Gell-Mann was elderly, vigorous, bright.
He had white hair, glasses with heavy dark rims, and a direct
manner. I explained the broad-ranging program that we had.
He was not interested.

"What are you doing to protect biodiversity?" he asked
pointedly. "I'm really only interested in biodiversity."

We finished lunch and I went back to my office in the art
deco Oviatt Building in downtown Los Angeles. I was pricked
by Gell-Mann's challenge. I decided to respond to it. But
how? We were a handful of lawyers and scientists, already
overcommitted. The biodiversity that interested me was
in the coastal areas. How could we stop the immensely
well funded juggernaut of Southern California coastal development?

Taking up this familiar question again, I applied a new
method. Instead of thinking through policy options and political realities, I began to meditate on it. While I had been meditating for some eight years at that point, I had never applied
it to solving a problem that was quintessentially legal. Seeing
no other way, though, I quieted the mind and let myself visu-
alize the area that I wanted to protect. As I visited the undeveloped land in my mind, I noticed a feature I had never
thought about before. There was a very clear coastal zone
that went from the ocean to the first ridge of hills. This clear
visual understanding of a coastal zone led to the next piece of
the puzzle. I became certain that there had to be a bird or a
mammal that lived only in that zone. Not a rat or lizard,
either. A species that had more charisma. If I could identify

one and get the federal government to list it as an endangered species, federal law would require certain protections. We would then be in a position to negotiate the protection of the coastal zone and its biodiversity with the land's owners and developers.

I left the meditation with the conviction that there would be a bird that met my need, though I did not know of one. I began to make phone calls to experts on Southern California fauna. Soon I was talking to John Atwood, an ornithologist at the Manomet Bird Observatory in Massachusetts. He had my bird. It turns out that he had completed a thick monograph on the California gnatcatcher not long before.

The gnatcatcher was the perfect creature for me: it lived in the coastal zone from Los Angeles to the Mexican border. Even better, it lived *only* in the coastal zone, from the shoreline up to the first ridgetop. It was sensitive to habitat disturbance and so was genuinely endangered, though it had not been listed as such. Atwood had done all the scientific background work we needed. Moreover, he knew the federal biologists who would have to pass on a petition for listing, and they were sympathetic.

Suddenly we had a case. If the gnatcatcher was not overtly charismatic, at least it was more so than the fringe-toed lizard or the snail darter. Nor was the Irvine Company, the largest landowner in California, in a position to cry poor. It was no logger who could claim to be put out of work by a bird.

With a legal intern named Mike Thrift, I put together a petition for listing the gnatcatcher as an endangered species. Within a week after we had filed the petition, I was off to Orange County, California, for a meeting with the Irvine Company, which was developing the coastline.

I drove down to Irvine with Mary Nichols, my partner in the office, who went on to become assistant administrator of the Environmental Protection Agency for the Clinton administration. One of our aims was to enter into a planning process with the landowners that was fair to all parties and to avoid the acrimony all too common in endangered species cases. Instead of focusing on the gnatcatcher alone, we wanted to plan for the protection of its habitat and for all of the species that live there—what gets too abstractly called biodiversity.

We began a process that day that is still going on. It was soon cited by Interior Secretary Bruce Babbitt as a national model for complex habitat-protection planning. Much work remains. But the posture of things has shifted. Moreover, over 325,000 acres have now been protected by agreement among all the parties in the first successful consensus planning process in the country.

These three stories all involve making room for creative intuition and being filled by it. The personalities of the people involved differ greatly. The problems they sought to solve differ greatly. Nevertheless, the method they used was similar, and it worked across all the differences. Why?

The physicist David Bohm argued that matter, mind, and energy form a mutually interactive ensemble. According to Bohm, all visible things—the explicate order—emerge together out of an ungraspable source of being which is beyond the rules of space and time—the implicate order. In this way of seeing things, our invitation to creative intuition is powerful indeed.

Bohm would allow that when we focus clearly on a problem and open ourselves to its solution, we create a kind of gravity well in space and time that attracts material from the implicate order to fill it. Everything needed for our answer crosses space and time instantaneously. Our question has the power to call its solution out of the heart of being.

Bohm's is a powerful description because he built it within the framework of physics, of which he was a consummate master. This kind of explanation allows us to relax the control of our analytic faculties by affording a well-built harbor they can tie up in for a while. The Eureka Practice requires that we put aside our analytic apparatus until the end of the process, when we then apply it with full force to our results. When we let in analysis too early, our best inspirations turn to dust in our hands.

Let us recall the Eureka Principle: A way out is always looking for a way in. As we look for creative solutions, we need only make the right kind of invitation, since a way out of our dilemma is always looking for a way into our mind.

The steps in the Eureka Practice are these:

1. Be absolutely clear about the problem.
2. Know all the relevant facts.
3. Know all the relevant rules.
4. Ask the question with absolute sincerity.
5. Go into silence until the answer emerges.
6. Test the answer analytically before proclaiming it.

1. **Be absolutely clear about the problem.** A fuzzy problem will not find a solution. Gandhi did not ask "How can I win a revolution?" He asked "In these circumstances, what nonviolent action can I take in the next few weeks that will galvanize the nation into nonviolent action?"

2. **Know all the relevant facts.** Unless you are a master of the facts, the problem is not specific enough to be solved. McClintock knew every corn plant. She knew every kernel on every corncob, many thousands of kernels. She knew exactly what each one represented. She then sought an answer to a specific anomalous pattern within the massive factual pattern that was clear to her mind. She did not wonder about genetics vaguely. The facts were perhaps clearer to her mind than they had ever been to anyone.

3. **Know all the relevant rules**. Unless you are a master of the rules, you have not built a channel into which a solution can flow. In the gnatcatcher case, I had extensive environmental law experience. I knew all the laws that might help me protect the coastal land I wanted to save. I knew them well enough to have an instinctual feel, almost a physical feel, for which ones might help and which ones would not.

4. **Ask the question with absolute sincerity**. This step is the turning point of the practice. The first three steps build your receiving station. But this step is your radio signal out into the source of being. To receive an answer, you must really want it with your whole being. Ask your question with your waking mind. Ask it as you enter dreams at night. You have to put your whole life into the demand for an answer. Then there is no resisting you. Across all space and time, an answer emerges from the Plenum. Without absolute sincerity, nothing happens.

5. **Go into silence until the answer emerges**. If there is static in your receiving station, you cannot receive an answer clearly. Stay in inner silence and you will recognize what comes. How long should you wait? Until you get the answer. Gandhi waited six weeks, most of it in silence. His was a big question. The experience in the McClintock and gnatcatcher stories is more typical. After a large investment of time and energy in the first four steps, the fifth may often take only a few lucid minutes, if you are ready. The amount of time does not matter when you really need the answer.

6. **Test the answer analytically before proclaiming it**. When an answer comes, remember that you are still in the practice. Test the answer. McClintock went back to her lab. I tested my intuition by talking to scientists and then to other lawyers. Gandhi must have thought and talked his action through too. I expect he got to this stage several times during the six weeks, tested his answers, rejected them, and began again.

Do not worry about beginning again. You are not using up a finite resource, after all, but calling on the formless source. Keep going until the answer holds up to the toughest test you can give it. Unless it holds up, you do not want to invest your life in it. And that is why you are asking in the first place.

Keep going.

5

The Way
of the Heart

Introducing the Way

The heart waits to open to the soul and to be filled with all the soul's knowing. It yearns to tear the membrane of separation we feel between us and what is real. It waits until we are willing to withdraw our attention from the everyday and focus it inward. The beat of our heart gives life and motion to our entire inner landscape. Let us listen to its rhythms.

The great systole and diastole of the heart are offering and asking. In the practice of offering we open everything we are, everything we have hidden from ourselves all our life long, and offer it to that which is greater than ourselves. In so doing we learn of it for the first time, in a way that is without threat or blame. We then work to liberate it, and in so doing we liberate ourselves. In the practice of asking, we ask for absolute fulfillment in that which is ultimately real. And when we ask, it begins to come.

The mind sees the wavelike nature of reality, the arising and falling of thought, feeling, pain, and all other experience. But like light, what we perceive in practice has a dual quality. For the heart, there are not waves but entities. The mind seeks the Ungraspable, and will in time relax its grip to let the Ungraspable pour in. The heart seeks communion with its Source, with the Other. This communion will come and the heart will meet the Other. Along the way, it will meet other entities—all the Beasts that dwell in the forests of the heart.

We yearn to have the smallest movement of our heart acknowledged, appreciated, and known before we need to speak it. We yearn for a wordless communion in the depths of silence with the source of all being, for a relationship of absolute commitment in which there is no hesitation and no shame attached to our most secret truths and most vile urgings. We yearn to be taught how to follow the steps that lead to our own happiness and the happiness of others. We yearn for the unwavering patience that picks us up every time we fall and gives us the courage to go on. We yearn to be understood, known, accepted, and loved.

This relationship of absolute love returned absolutely is our birthright and is waiting for us. We can live in it, in the midst of the world and all its demands. It is this relationship that the heart leads us into, in its own time, when we give it room to do so.

Offering

Let us take the first step into the practice of offering. For many of us, this first step will be the hardest part.

Sit comfortably and follow your breath. Relax into your breath completely, and let yourself feel the breath as it fills your lungs and as your lungs empty. Your lungs are to air as your heart is to blood.

Let yourself feel the way your lungs surround and support your heart. Lungs breathing, moving in and out as the heart beats. From awareness of breath to awareness of the heart. Let your attention move to the heart and rest there. Remember to stay in your body. Mystical experience happens to us in the body. We need to stay aware of it always.

As your attention rests on the heart, allow yourself to feel your yearning to connect with the ultimate source of love. Let the yearning emerge in all of its strength. If it happens naturally, let the yearning have a quality of absoluteness, yearning for absolute love given absolutely.

As this yearning comes forward, ask to whom you should direct it. The heart personalizes its messages. Is there a divine being to whom you can direct it? An

entity greater than yourself with whom you can speak,
be heard and understood?

You may find it easy to know to whom to send the
yearning. Or you may encounter resistance. You may
encounter great resistance. If pain comes forward,
invite it in and work with it. If pain comes forward, it
needs to be heard. When the yearning carries pain, the
pain needs release before the yearning can flow.

LETTING THE YEARNING FLOW

When I first began to do heart practice I met fierce resistance.
I had spent long years training and taking refuge in my
mind. I believed in no invisible entities I could talk to. That
is why I liked the way of the mind. Tough, clear, seeing
through things: everything seen as a wave emerging from the
Plenum.

There was also a side of me that needed to work directly
with feelings in some way I could not specify. I wanted to
meet the beasts in the forests of my heart. I knew that I had
to search for them and that I would have to cross a threshold
I had never crossed before the search could begin. I crossed
that threshold in an atelier in a little German village. I had
gone there for a solo retreat that wound up lasting fourteen
months. For the first couple of months, I practiced the way of
the mind assiduously, sitting nine hours a day. Then the urge
arose to test the way of the heart. I felt embarrassed. When
practicing the way of the mind, I felt like a physicist at work.
When I thought of the way of the heart it seemed sticky, full
of delusions, a labyrinth of myth and nonsense I would lose
myself in.

Nevertheless, the time had come to put my fears and
doubts aside. I locked my door, sat in my room, and prayed.
When I started to pray, great resistance arose to meet me. A

powerful anger and sense of betrayal came forward. I had
believed in God as a boy, only to feel betrayed. Where had
this God gone? Despite all attempts to understand myself,
nothing like a God was apparent or gave any discernible help.
Why should I put energy now into what I knew was fantasy?
Why fool myself?

I also felt a tremendous desire to connect with the Divine
that had been bottled up for many years. I let this carry forward the anger and sense of betrayal. I let them concentrate
and condense the pain from all those many years. In that atelier, I finally directed the anger explicitly at God. If I were
going to have a relationship with God, it had to be one in
which I could let all of my feelings out and be heard. If polite-
ness was required, or piety, I was not interested.

So I let the anger flow. I railed aloud at God for more than
three hours. Passionately, loudly. I shouted and I wept. I left
nothing unsaid. "I doubt You exist, but life is not worth living
unless you do!" I screamed, astonished to hear myself voice
this. I argued that my youthful devotion had been betrayed
by the Catholic Church. I opened a lifetime's pain and let
myself feel the reservoir of pain that each of us has but that
we shut off to get on with life. For twenty-five years, I had not
been able to think of a Divine without running into a wall in
my mind and heart. A heavy wall, black, nonporous, impene-
trable, between my experience and whatever God was. I knew
no way of piercing it. Until that day in that room.

After more than three hours, I was exhausted. All my
points were made, all my arguments given. The only thing left
was to offer it all. To give myself completely in my honesty
and to see if anything would come of it. I was still skeptical. I
said, "If You are real, I give the rest of my life to You. I give
You this pain, I give You this betrayal, I give You all these feelings. All this yearning, all this exhaustion, all the feeling of
having wasted the last twenty-five years. All the loneliness of

those years. I give them all to You completely. They are Yours now. I have had them long enough and am tired of them. I cannot carry on in this way any longer. I insist on something else! Life has to be better than this! I give You all my pain and alienation. It is Yours now. You deal with it! I have had enough of living like this! If You are real, show me, enter into a relationship with me, come forward now. I have nothing left to hide and nothing left to give."

At that moment, I felt a phenomenally powerful charge of energy explode in my head, like a lightning bolt hitting a tree in a thunderstorm in the middle of the night. Huge, overpowering, out of scale, and out of nowhere. Frightening and exciting at once. The energy ran to ground through my body. Running along the nerve fibers, it lit up their ten thousand branching filaments throughout the whole body. I felt them all come alive in a jolt that penetrated every cell.

I was astonished. I did not know what to make of it. My mind could find no explanation. The impervious black wall of separation was so strong, however, that the skepticism held. I might have imagined the discharge of energy, I told myself. I might have so strongly wanted a response that I induced it. So I said, speaking again to God, "I may have caused this experience. If You are real, do it again now!"

And in that moment a second dazzling discharge of energy came. Again lightning branched through me as it hit. Had the room been dark, the lightning would have lit it up like high noon in the desert.

I started to pray over the next few days for the connection to deepen. Each time I did so, I felt energy jolt into me and suffuse my whole body. This happened not once or twice but thirty or forty times a day. Nothing in my experience or anything I had read made sense of what was happening. I could find out only by going forward.

After a few days of prayer, the answer began to change. It

would not come every time I prayed. The lightning would not answer. Then I would get panicky. The desire for connection would flow anew. The electric answer would jolt into me again as soon as the desire for connection clarified.

I saw that the electric answer came only in response to a true desire for connection—a genuine aspiration. I realized that Someone or Something was listening to the innermost movements of my heart. I felt unalone for the first time since I was a boy. Here was the Divine, listening and answering right in my nervous system. There was no other way to see it. The astonishing series of lightning bolts had attacked and broken down the black wall of separation in my consciousness. This experience was the pivot on which my whole life turned. There was simply no room for doubt anymore: there was a Force, Presence, Light, and Power, and I could enter into the most intimate relationship with It.

One warm summer night soon thereafter, I was walking in the countryside, and I prayed for a sign that what I was experiencing was real. A moment later, a shooting star appeared in the sky just ahead of me. I thought it beautiful. I thought it perhaps a coincidence. And I prayed, "If this is the sign, let me be given another shooting star."

I was given five, one after another, again and again. I could only laugh, offer thanks, and head up the hill toward home. I did not think a Divine had sent planetesimals hurtling through the atmosphere solely for my benefit. But I was stunned again by the rapprochement between my heart's needs and the real.

DEEPENING THE PRACTICE

Let us return to heart practice. The yearning for connection with the source of being breaks down all barriers. We need only let it flow.

*Sit comfortably and enter into silence. Be fully present
in your body. Let everything relax into stillness. When
it has, then call the yearning forth.*

*Recognize it, name it, and let it carry you. It is the
river that will carry you across to the other side. It is
the energy that will rise to break through the walls
around your heart. It is the talisman that makes travel
anywhere in the inner landscape perfectly safe.*

*This yearning is itself already the way home. Just to
let it flow is to know that there is a home for the heart,*
' *and also a way home.*

My experience was so strong precisely because my barrier,
the black wall of separation, was so old, calcified, and thick
that it needed a powerful force to open a crack in it.

As you go into the practice, let yourself identify the entity
you feel comfortable addressing. It may be the Divine, a saint,
the living Earth, Gaia. It may be Christ. It may be the Plenum,
from which all things emerge. For one of my students, it was
Salmon, the spirit of these great free swimming beings.

The entity you address needs to be a being greater than
yourself, and one that you feel an intimate relationship with
or the potential for an intimate relationship with. Close
enough to address it and be heard.

*Let yourself continue to sit in silence, feeling your
heart. Take the time to find the entity to address.*

*If you need to wrestle with God, now is the time to
do it. So turn off the phone, lock your door, and wrestle with Him or Her or It. Do not stop until you reach
completion.*

*Do not stop until you are satisfied that you can
address a being greater than yourself and be heard.
Until you have this satisfaction, the practice cannot
move deeper.*

When you are ready, you can begin to offer your whole life. You can offer everything in the body, the emotions, and the mind. Everything in the entire life.

People often tell me they do not know how to offer. It is the most natural thing in the world when you get the hang of it. So let us look at some examples from a normal day.

How to Get Up and Get Through the Day

The way of the mind uses awareness to bring us into our bodies. The way of the heart adds offering. The practice of offering brings us into our bodies in a profound way that can touch old wounds and heal them.

GETTING UP:

Everything in the field of the body can be offered. Everything that the body is or does. Let us start by looking at the first hour of the day.

> As you lie in bed after waking, feel your breath and follow it into your body. Become aware of your whole body. Do not move it. Just be aware of it. This takes only a moment.
>
> When you are aware of your whole body, then offer it. Use your own words, as if you were a child talking with its loving mother. Let yourself move into the relaxation that brings spontaneity.
>
> Let the mind be quiet, as yet unhurried by the day and its demands. Then say in your own words, in the realm of inner silence, something simple, like: "I give You my body completely, and I give You everything

that it will do today. Help me remember You today through everything my body does."

Over time, you can let this morning offering evolve into something like this:

"I give You my body, mind, and soul completely. Enjoy Yourself through all of me today."

The secret behind offering lies in remembering that there is Someone who can receive whatever we offer. As we offer, remembrance comes naturally and the sense of separation wears thin. Then all of life fills with wonder.

So you are lying in bed in the morning. You have already offered the whole body, and by now you have stretched and gotten up. As you go to the toilet, be aware of what you do. We often rush through these actions and treat them as unimportant. In doing so, we treat ourselves as unimportant. When we pay full attention to our actions instead, we begin to heal ourselves.

USING THE TOILET:

By simply using the toilet with full awareness, we can appreciate the body, the psyche, and the soul, all functioning harmoniously.

As you enter the bathroom, be fully conscious of what you do. Bring your awareness into play and enter the moment, with no thought about your tasks for the day.
Feel yourself fully present in your body. As you use the toilet, say in your heart: "I offer this to You."

If you feel this attention and this offering are inappropriate or sacrilegious, note that feeling and offer it. Let it go.

Stay in the feeling of the heart. The heart lives always in the present moment. For the heart, everything we do is sacred.

As you experiment, you will see that everything can be offered. When we offer everything, it is not to make it sacred but to recognize the inherent sacredness in every gesture, waiting to be revealed to our sight. There is no separation.

What you are most ashamed of, what seems darkest, is precisely what is most precious to offer. By offering it, we reclaim a part of ourselves that was lost in the shadows of shame, guilt, or some other negative force. Whenever anything that is dark arises, offer it. It arises to seek your help. It arises so that you can, by offering it, release it into light.

HAVING BREAKFAST:

Continue offering everything you do as you go through the morning.

> *Before you eat breakfast, pause for a moment and silently offer the food you eat: "I offer this food to You." Very simple. When you remember in this way, you may feel gratitude flow.*
>
> *As you eat breakfast, be fully aware of breakfast. Follow your breath into your body. Be fully present in your body. Place your full awareness on the taste of the food.*
>
> *Reflect, too, on all the labors of the people, animals, and plants that contributed to your nourishment.*
>
> *How can we not feel grateful?*

We usually do not take even a moment to feel the gratitude that naturally comes to us from having food to eat. Offering our food allows the gratitude to be perfected in a moment of time. This feeling, too, is an experience of no separation.

LEAVING THE HOUSE:

If you live with someone, or have a family, hug them before you leave for work. Hold them gently.

> *Feel your heart in your chest as you hold them. Be aware of the love in your heart and let it flow freely into their heart as you hold them to yours. A full and free flow of love without boundaries.*
>
> *Your heart is a Sun, radiating love. As is their heart. Feel the warmth from their heart, commingling with yours and filling your body.*
>
> *As you do this, offer it, gently and silently: "I offer this to You."*

If your companions are cats or dogs, you can use this practice with them too. It is easy to feel their love. If you live alone, offer your love to your house or apartment and to whatever is there that is precious to you. It may be to the fern you carefully tend or to the spirit of the place. When you do this, you will find your home welcoming when you return.

As you go to work, be aware of all the physical sensations of driving, walking, or taking the subway. Offer them simply: "I offer these to You." Note any feeling that arises on the way to work. It may be boredom, elation, anger, depression, or some mix of feelings you cannot name. Whatever the contents of the feelings, offer them.

> *Say in your heart for the boredom, "I offer this to You."*
> *Say in your heart for the elation, "I offer this to You."*
> *Say in your heart for the anger, "I offer this to You."*
> *Say in your heart for the depression, "I offer this to You."*
>
> *When you cannot name your feelings, say in your*

heart, "I offer You all these confused feelings that I can-
not name. I give them to You; take them now."

Carry on this practice throughout the day. It is not intru-
sive, it takes no time away from anything you need to do. On
the contrary, it creates a feeling of spaciousness in a busy day
by repeatedly opening the awareness to a presence much
greater than our own.

GETTING THROUGH THE DAY:

Every day brings its satisfactions, its stresses, its dramas. Each
of them brings with it a field of feelings. Our experience of
the day is nothing other than what we encounter as we traverse these fields of feelings we find in our inscape. We can
offer them all.

If you are following the way of the mind, you are watching feelings as they arise through the day. You are residing in
spaciousness and watching them as a naturalist. The way of
the heart fits together seamlessly at this point with the way of
the mind. When a feeling arises, we can become aware of it,
name it, and offer it, whatever it is.

We will work with some difficult feelings. But as you go
through the day, remember to offer your positive feelings too.
Offer the impulses of your heart. Offer the flowers on a distant mountain. Offer a little triumph. Offer a daydream. Offer
your wish to be somewhere more exotic. Offer a pleasing sexual charge. Offer the emerald-green algae on an iceberg off
the Arctic coast. Offer whatever moves you in each moment,
and you will find more and more that moves you.

HAVING LUNCH:

Back now to our rounds of the day. You may find yourself in
a busy delicatessen waiting for a sandwich, in a great rush

because you have a project with a deadline waiting on your desk. The person on line in front of you will almost certainly decide that he or she needs to have a long conversation or a heated argument with the person behind the counter, whose attention you are waiting for.

What do you feel in this situation? If you are irritable like me, you will feel judgment arise toward the people holding you up. "How could they be so stupid, so inconsiderate . . ." Not far behind judgment is anger: "Dammit, I don't have all day to wait here while this idiot . . ."

How do you offer these feelings? Again, it is simple.

Follow your breath into your body. Become aware of your feelings. Notice how they feel in your body. Is your stomach clutched, your diaphragm tense? Let yourself feel the full extent of the stress in your body. It takes only a moment.

When you have done this, move to your heart. Move there even if it is difficult to do, because you would rather make a sarcastic comment to the person in line ahead of you or fume silently.

Feeling your heart, and the stress in your body and feelings, offer it: "I offer all this mess to You!" It is easy to mean it when you say it.

Once you have taken a moment to notice the stress in your body, you become acutely aware that you would prefer to let the stress go. Offering it is a powerful way to do that. It puts spaciousness around the stress. It acknowledges that we are more than our stress and that our reach is broader than the annoyance of the moment. It allows us to transform a situation that is stressful into one that connects us with the source of our being.

As you go through your ordinary day, be systematic about offering your feelings. Every time annoyance comes up, offer it. Every time something stressful comes up, offer it. Every

time someone else's drama spills over messily into your life,
offer the slop.

SITTING IN A MEETING:

We all have meetings to attend. While we are sitting in a
meeting, it can seem we spend our whole life attending
meetings. How can we work with the whole of a meeting
and any difficulties we face in it? Simply by offering them.
When we do this, we perform an alchemy in which what dis-
turbs and isolates us serves instead to reconnect us with our
source.

When you go into a meeting, whether you are eager for it
or would prefer to be elsewhere:

Say silently, in your heart, "I offer this to You."

When you are irritated by hearing the same person make
the same point in the same narrow-minded way:

Say silently, in your heart, "I offer this to You."

When you carry your point in a discussion, and when you
are humiliated:

Say silently, in your heart, "I offer this to You."

When the meeting ends:

Say silently, in your heart, "I offer this to You."

There is a tremendous amount of time in meetings to
use the offering practice. Human communication is rich
with redundancy. When you listen with full awareness, time
opens up. A pearl of new information will be followed by a

long string of old news. Use the spaces between pearls to offer everything that is going on both within and without you. Your frustration and boredom will go into diminuendo, and the fresh music of the present moment will fill you instead.

USING THE TELEPHONE:

The telephone can be a wonderful instrument of practice as we go through the day. I discovered this at the NRDC law office in Los Angeles. The phone would ring almost constantly. The person on the other end of the line always had a problem. It could be a colleague upset about something, a defense lawyer who wanted to argue, someone from the head office wanting me to raise more money, a board member wanting me to focus on his or her needs. All the normal things everyone in business faces every day.

Because the phone rang all day, I found it distracted me from what I wanted to do: the calls I wanted to make; briefs I wanted to write; strategies I wanted to plan, and so on. I began to experience an internal twinge whenever the phone rang. This was a problem. It neither made me happy nor made it any easier to take care of the needs of the people who were calling. Something had to be done.

I began to let the phone call me into calmness. Using a practice I had learned from the Buddhist monk Thich Nhat Hanh, I began to let it ring three times when it rang, rather than picking it up on the first ring. I breathed three times as the phone rang, and then offered the experience I was about to have, whatever it was, as I raised the receiver.

What a difference this made. Soon I experienced the phone as something that brought moments of stress-reducing awareness into my day. One of the secretaries started to come into my office periodically and sit near the phone. After a few days I asked her why she was doing this. She said, "When I need to get calm, I like to come in and just sit by your telephone for a little while."

You can practice with the phone like this:

When the telephone rings, become aware of the ringing, but do not move to lift the receiver. Instead, let it ring three times before answering. On each ring, breathe, and follow your breath into your body.

Become fully aware of your breath, fully present in your body. Just the breath, just the body.

On the fourth ring, move to pick up the receiver. As you do so, say in your heart, "I offer this to You. Whoever this is, whatever I am about to experience, I offer it to You."

COOKING DINNER:

As we cook we touch the good things of the Earth, to welcome them into our bodies. Cooking is grounding and relaxing. Cooking is an act of love with the Earth and with those we feed. When we give our full awareness to our cooking, we make our love into a tangible thing, nourishing and tasty.

Everything we need to know can be found in chopping an onion.

As you get ready to chop an onion, follow your breath into your body. Feel your breath, feel your body. Become aware of your hands and arms. As you begin to chop, feel your body working rhythmically, perfectly: body, onion, Earth. Life flowing into life without the need of thought.

Smell the perfume released by the onion, that amazing, odiferous lily. Acknowledge the thousands of species of lilies growing all over the Earth, in her rich and living soils. Feel the riotous vegetable profusion of the growing blooming Earth, feeding all living beings, all condensed into the onion beneath your hands.

Feel the knife move through the layers of the onion's tender body, layer after layer releasing its secrets. Feel the connection between hungry humans and humble onions through the millennia, and let yourself connect with your ancestors in this way. Let yourself feel that you share one body with your ancestors, all of us nourished by the Earth. All of us children of the Earth, fed and taken care of.

And then: "I offer this to You."

You can in this way offer everything you do through each stage of preparing the meal and opening a bottle of wine. Before you taste the wine:

"I offer this to You."

The wine thus offered will grow in depth, and its effect, too, will be connection with the Earth, the source of all goodness and nourishment. Remember to offer your meal before you eat it. And then relish it. Relish it as the purest form of gratitude. So whether you are eating alone or sharing food with those you love, *Bon appetit!*

TAKING CARE OF THE NEEDS OF A SPOUSE OR PARTNER:

If we are fortunate enough to have a spouse or partner, we will certainly experience times of difficulty when thoughts and feelings arise that we wish would go away. The other person may be sick or growing old, or may be having trouble with work, an addiction, or in some other way need special support.

When another person with whom we share our life needs help, we give it, but we need to be aware of how we give it.

We can easily give away too much of ourselves, too much of our energy, in a way that is not good for either person in the long run. The sustained giving that is compassion requires that we take care of our own vital needs first.

We can easily forget our own needs when the needs of the other are compelling. How can we tell if we have neglected our own needs? By listening to our feelings. We may be surprised to find that we get irritated by the person we are helping, even though we love that person. We may go beyond irritation to anger. We may go beyond anger and have fantasies of murder.

Such thoughts and feelings will horrify us at first. We will try to push them away, take vigorous walks to get them out of our system, tell ourselves that we are good people and simply do not have such feelings. And yet the truth is that we may.

When we have such feelings, we need to acknowledge them. Though they seem threatening, they are helpful messengers of our own needs. Violence is done by people who do not let their feelings arise into view and so take care of them. When we take care of them, feelings cannot harm us or take control of us.

We are all familiar with the safety lecture we get when we fly. The stewardess reminds us that if the plane has difficulties, and the oxygen masks appear before us, we should put our own masks on first. Then and only then, she will tell us, should we help children and old people near us to put their oxygen masks on. If we try to help them first, without assuring our own supply of oxygen, we may pass out, and then both of us may die.

As a painful feeling toward your partner begins to trouble you, become aware of it. Then move to your breath. Feel your breath. Follow your breath into your body.

Become fully present to your breath, fully present in your body.

When you are fully present in the body, invite the feeling in. "Whoever you are, I know you have something to teach me. Come forward now, and teach me what I need to know."

Stay present to the breath, present in the body. Let the feeling come, and look into it. Stay with it and investigate it. What does it have to teach? Say to the feeling: "What do you have to teach me?"

As you look into the feeling, remaining present to your breath and present in your body, the inner nature of the feeling will reveal itself. It is part of yourself that needs attention, and when you give it your attention, it will tell you what it needs. Listen to it. It may take only a little while, or you may have to listen to it in visits spread over several days. After you have listened to it, however long that takes, you are then ready to offer it:

"I offer this feeling to You. Take it now, and give me the love, strength, and wisdom I need to take care of myself and of my partner, now and for the rest of my life. Show me how to take care of us both in a good and healthy way."

When you offer difficult feelings, you begin to feel them move. When they move, you feel the stress associated with them diminish. As you do this practice more, the results are sometimes dramatic. There will be times when you become aware of anger and offer it, and feel it lift like a veil being raised, seconds after you offer it. There is sometimes a blissful feeling of energy that descends to replace the anger that you have offered and released.

For this practice to work, you need to make it completely your own. As you practice with it at first, it is like practicing the piano by playing scales. As you experiment with it throughout the day, you will soon be playing real music. Become an artist of your own life. This art is gentle and playful. It is never grim, even when we are exhausted. When you play with the practice in this way, its effects are self-reinforcing. You experience the value of the practice, and so continue to enjoy playing with it and finding new ways to use it.

One day I was standing in a newspaper store in London. A situation arose that would usually irritate me: I was kept waiting while the storekeeper chatted with a friend. Instead of irritation, however, I felt a lovely soft energy descending and filling me. I had to stop and laugh at myself when I realized what was happening. The irritation had arisen as usual, but offering it had become so automatic that I was unaware of having done it. So I only felt the results of the practice: the soft energy replacing the irritation. This kind of experience becomes a normal one for us.

MAKING LOVE:

Making love is a joyful exchange of offerings with our partner. We can offer this intimacy to the source of our being as well. When we do, the entire experience is enriched. We begin to feel that we are in an eternal love triangle. Facing our partner, we are the bottom two corners of the triangle, which extends up to include the Eternal Source. Our love moves from two dimensions in ordinary time to three dimensions in timeless time, when we remember to offer it.

As you make love, be fully present in the body, fully present in the moment. Let all fantasies go, and dwell in the astonishing presence of your partner.

Be fully present to the body of your lover in your arms. Body, psyche, soul all present in you both, all exciting, all ravishing, all an astonishing gift.

Let your heart open fully, and feel yourself give and receive love without boundaries.

Express this love in a thousand ways, giving and receiving, nourishing and being nourished, pleasuring and being pleasured.

When you have an orgasm, say silently in your heart, "I offer this to You."

When we offer our love, we feel the birth of our love into the dimension of eternity. It becomes everyday magic. Our relationship begins to go easier and smoother. We begin to look to our partners for our human needs and stop burdening them with our absolute needs.

Our absolute needs begin to flow to the Absolute. All the problems of a relationship then become easier to move through. We begin to see them in a new and enormous context: they become opportunities for growth into a maturing relationship with each other and the Absolute.

No problem we face seems too large when we experience it in this context. Offering our love for our partner, offering our relationship, offering ourselves. When we offer in this way, we receive so much more than we give that we never stop offering.

GOING TO SLEEP:

As you prepare to go to sleep, take a moment to complete the day and prepare for tomorrow by offering it all. Offer the whole day, and all your joys and troubles in it. Offer tomorrow, and all your hopes and expectations. Offer your sleep and dreams and everything that will happen in them.

As you lie in bed, become aware of your breath. Follow your breath into your body. Become fully aware of your breath, fully present in your body. Offer your whole day. Let it flash through your mind, and as it does so, say in your heart, "I offer You this."

Let yourself feel any feelings you have about tomorrow, and as they move through: "I offer You this."

As you move toward sleep: "I offer You my body, mind, and soul. Use them for Your purposes while I sleep."

We have now completed a day in which everything has been offered. When we offer in this global way, everything we meet is transformed into the material of our awakening. As we persist in this practice, we learn little by little, through the humble tutelage of daily life, to be intimate with ourselves. Our perspective shifts, and we realize that we were never separate from the source of our being; we only thought we were.

MOVING BEYOND OBSESSION AND SELF-JUDGMENT

In the way of the mind, we become conscious of the nature of our thoughts, rising into consciousness like waves and like waves receding. We gain a clarity of view and become aware of what we judge harshly and of our obsessive patterns of thought.

Once we become aware of harsh judgments that repeat themselves, how do we work with them? This is a place where the way of the heart completes the way of the mind. Let us consider obsessive thoughts. Common areas include sex, power, and money. I remember reading the results of a psychological study in which young men were asked to keep track of what they were thinking during a typical day. They made a note in a journal every fifteen minutes as the day went on. What emerged was that for fully 40 percent of their mental time, the men were having sexual fantasies.

There is nothing wrong in that. The question is only how we want to spend this precious human life. The same question arises as to power, money, or anything else. How much of our life do we spend obsessing about power, money, or whatever else arises frequently into our consciousness? It may be thoughts about being fashionable or ugly, brilliant or incompetent, macho or sickly, rich or a failure, beautiful or fat, or any number of other things. In all of these thoughts, which so color our psychology, there is a powerful set of attachments, giving impulse to their cycling through our minds. We can simply continue to let these attachments rise and fall, filling our minds with obsessive thoughts. Or we can take action. What action can we take? Very simple, says the way of the heart. Offer them.

Obsessive thoughts are like dandelions. They have deep roots that we cannot easily pull. So offer them root and all when they arise. This does not imply condemning them or yourself for having them arise within you. On the contrary. We observe the thoughts like a naturalist. We offer them to let them move and to free our mental and emotional space from their influence. No condemnation necessary. Just getting on with business.

So when we obsess about sex, money, or whatever else, we note the thoughts arising and offer them. Together with all the weedy roots that proliferate below them. As we do this again and again, we begin to get some space around them; we can see them coming at us across our inscape from some distance, instead of finding out about their visit by waking up and realizing that we are already in the midst of living out an obsessive pattern. We can work similarly with judgmental thoughts, which are one of the great sources of unhappiness in our lives. However harshly we may judge others, this is only a warm-up exercise for judging ourselves. Every time we do this, we erect another filter within ourselves that reduces our ability to know love. The more we judge ourselves, the more miserable we become.

How can we break this cycle? Very simple, says the way of the heart again. Offer the judgment. Become aware of it as it arises and then offer it. To touch the harshness of judgment with the tenderness of offering is to perform a small miracle of kindness toward ourselves.

Over time, we discover that the offering practice works on self-judgment in a deeper way than we at first imagine. It penetrates to the roots like a healing balm. As we offer all of the most difficult material in our lives and begin to feel it move, we realize that the entity to whom we are offering it really is accepting it. If She or He is accepting it, there is no judging us for having these thoughts, feelings, and experiences.

When this understanding hits in a visceral way, it sets off a powerful explosion of self-acceptance that propels us beyond self-judgment. For if the Divine is not judging me for being who I am, how can I judge myself for it?

The Divine is happy for us to bare our wounds. In the moment when we reveal them, we see It has no judgment about them. And yet only when we reveal them to ourselves can our wounds be healed. We need to admit everything that we have been hoping would go away if we ignore it. When we ignore wounds, they fester. When we ignore our shadows, they feed on our vital energy and do whatever they have to do to get our attention, so they get their chance of melting into light.

In offering, we are acknowledging to ourselves what needs healing and offering it for healing. As we heal our wounds, we gain the freedom to be ourselves. We gain confidence that we can walk into our shadows, reveal them to the light of our awareness, and release them into the greater light. When we see this, we lose all fear of revealing ourselves to ourselves, for we trust that we will meet ourselves with love instead of judgment.

SUMMARY OF THE OFFERING PRACTICE

As we have now seen, the offering practice works throughout the day with all the material of our lives. As we offer whatever troubles us, we are reconnected with our source. Troubles diminish into difficulties. We put aside self-judgment and live in the spontaneous revelation of life in the ever-present moment.

Offering is prayer. As we offer more and more, we begin to abide in the heart's precinct, from which all prayer emerges.

Asking

Asking is the reciprocal of offering; it is the complementary form of prayer. In offering, we offer all the landscape of our awareness. We offer the flowers of our consciousness and all the muck as well, everything that we have allowed to collect in the septic ponds of our inscape. As we do this we unify our experience: we come to know that all aspects of our experience must be brought out to meet the face of love. No part of our inscape is left separate, off-limits, closed to our exploration, renewal, and enjoyment.

Asking unifies our experience in a complementary way. It allows our aspiration for union, our will to resolve tension into love, to sink down and penetrate into all aspects of our being. In offering, we lift up what is dark and bring it into the light. By dark I do not mean evil. I mean everything that has not yet been clarified, that resists the transformative power of consciousness. A great deal of what we find in ourselves does that. In asking, we call down the light.

One of the great rules of consciousness is the rule about asking. The experience of consciousness is so exquisitely tuned to our freedom that we must ask for transformation before it comes. We must ask to be shown who we are. We must ask for our hearts to find union with the source of our being. We must ask to find the way.

When we ask with absolute sincerity, the way opens. There is no doubt of it. But we must ask. We must participate in the creation of our freedom. We must open ourselves to the experience of transformation by asking for it. We must take full responsibility for our own awareness. We must call the light to us.

When we ask for love, we are given love. When we ask for peace, we are given peace. When we ask to find the way, the way is made open to us. When we ask to grow, we are given what we need to grow. When we ask for complete union and realization, our life becomes a journey richer and more powerful than we have ever imagined. Opening leads to opening. The world fills with meaning. Our work becomes our play, and our play brings forward all our talents. Nothing that we have thought about it beforehand can touch it.

There are no restrictions that govern what we ask for. Why not ask for everything? Ask for the grace to fully realize who you are. This is what Jesus was talking about when he said, "Ask and you shall receive." When you ask for *that* it definitely begins to come. It comes in its own time, in its own rhythm, at the pace at which we can absorb it.

If you ask for the grace to realize who you are, ask also for the courage you will need to do so. To realize who you are, you will have to walk through all the shadows in your inner landscape. It is not easy. You will need to give up all your views about yourself again and again, each time they crystallize into a pattern. You will have to experience and release all the pain in your life. You will have to embrace your death. You will have to bear everything to realize everything. A perfect divine economy.

Calling Down
What You Need

The offering practice empties us of darkness; asking for transformation opens us. Now we will move to calling down what we need. Calling down what we need begins to fill us. Every human lover also knows this practice: to fill the mind with the object of longing. It is the natural movement of the heart in the theater of the sacred, too. We call on what the heart needs until we feel it come. Then we call in gratitude. There is nothing better we can do. In this way we enter into the romance of the Absolute.

At the beginning we may feel nothing. This will change if we let the yearning flow.

Let the heart's utmost yearning come forward.

Its yearning for immersion in the source of all being. Its yearning to dissolve in the ocean of love. Its yearning to know at last that it can never be alone and has never been alone. Its yearning to know the Absolute with the intimate touch of the lover. Its yearning to know it can call at all times, in all circumstances, about anything great or small, and be heard. Its yearning to know that beyond being heard, it is responded to, in ways that it can know and in ways it can never know.

Cuboards / Cab.

When the longing comes forward, condense it in a name. Remember that the heart personalizes. If you are a Christian you might use the Jesus prayer: "Lord Jesus Christ, have mercy on me." If you are an environmentalist, it might be Gaia. If you are a Hindu, it might be Krishna.

Let it be an entity that the heart can have a relationship with. If you can find no name, try Mother: the Mother of All Things; the Earth; the Plenum from which all being emerges; the gentle death that takes us home. Let Mother mean all these things and every other thing your heart yearns to connect with.

Mother. The source of all love. The source of confidence that there is meaning in this life. Mother. Let your deep instinctual love of your human mother help kindle the practice.

The love of our mother, which we can never fully understand, express enough gratitude for, or fully return. The love of our mother, which will forever be a mystery, which we can never forget, and which is present through all generations.

Let all the mammalian instinct for connection and care come forward. Let all the emotional need for intimacy and love come forward. Let all the mental need for understanding and support come forward. Let all the soul's need to complete its journey come forward.

Then begin to call on what the heart desires with that name. Call with the silence of the heart. "Mother." Or "Lord Jesus Christ, have mercy." Or "Gaia." Or whatever name comes to you for that which your heart desires union with.

Call on the name endlessly. This practice sustained the Desert Fathers in their lives as anchorites and it works just as well in city traffic.

Do not stint. Sail into the repetition of the name

with the excitement of charting unknown seas, where
great discoveries lie ahead. Because they do.
    Call on the name throughout the day. In the car, in
meetings, as you go through the ordinary affairs of the
day, call on the name. Let yourself relax into the call-
ing. Let it be as natural as the breath. You may also let
it follow the breath, if that is comfortable. Let it make
up the texture of the mind.

We become what we turn our minds to. If we endlessly
turn them to the source of love we become love. The source
of love and sustenance enters into our awareness throughout
the day, while ten thousand things conspire to throw us off
our course.

The ordinary stress of life pulls our untrained minds and
hearts away into distraction from the real. In calling on the
name, we are returning to our course again and again, like
checking a homing beacon or a signal light in dark and foggy
waters. In calling on the name, ten thousand things conspire
to keep us on our course.

When you have time to meditate, continue calling on the
name in your mind. A time will come when the mind naturally
falls silent. This is the reverence of the mind for the approach
of what we have called. When we call, we are heard. When
we call, that which we call comes. As we go more deeply into
the practice, we feel the approach of what we call.

As you use this practice, you may find that there is a natural transition in which another name begins to arise. I began
by using "Father" and then, after a few months and a deepen-
ing of experience, I changed to "Beloved."

"Beloved," completely empty, completely full. "Beloved,"
to return me to myself with all the power residing in the emotional body of a human being. "Beloved," to trust, and so complete the return. I say it in my heart and mind endlessly. After
doing this for some time, I found myself holding the name for

several beats. For a long time I did not know why these rhyth-
mic beats came into it, like this: "Be-lo-o-o-ved." But they
came, and so I followed. Years later I realized it was the
rhythm of my heart, beating out the name of what it needs,
naturally entraining my mind to its rhythm.

Follow your heart. It will show you what to call and also
bring it to you. Call on a name that points to the source of
being. Do this with absolute sincerity.

The Beasts in the Forests
of Our Hearts

The way of the heart takes us into the forests of our hearts. We go there to face the beasts that dwell in them. These beasts are the active manifestations of the shadows in our lives. All we are most attached to, all we most fear, all we most repress. Everything we are running from. We first experience these beasts as an external threat. As we come to know them, we realize they are the aspects of ourselves most in need of love.

Dante gives the archetypal description of the beasts. The *Inferno* opens with these lines, in a contemporary translation by Peter Thornton:

> When I had reached the midpoint of our life's
> journey, I found myself in a dark wood
> for I had lost the straight road. Ah, how hard
> a thing it is to tell what that was like,
> that wild, rough, and impenetrable forest,
> the very thought of which revives my fear!
>
> . . . .
>
> And all at once, near where the slope began
> to steepen, there appeared a leopard, agile
> and very quick, covered with spotted fur;
> and it would not depart but stayed before me,

*cutting my progress off to such a point
that more than once I turned to go back down.*

. . . .

*The figure of a lion
That now appeared before me filled me with fear.
It seemed that he was making straight towards me
with head held high and raging in his hunger,
making the very air appear to tremble.
And after him a wolf that in her leanness
seemed crammed with every craving, she had forced
numberless people to live in misery.
This one brought so much heaviness upon me,
inspiring fear in me with her appearance,
that I abandoned hope of reaching the top.*

In the middle of the journey of my life, I was drawn to the High Sierras and heard the voice that propelled me on my journey. The voice issued a challenge: "Do you have the courage for the solitude you need to face those beasts?" I did not at that time know what solitude was.

SOLITUDE

I had led an active life in the world. There were quiet evenings, solo day hikes, periods of intense study, and daily meditation. No real solitude, though. That came to me during the time I lived in Germany. When I arrived, I meditated for nine hours a day for the first six weeks or so. I lived without speaking to anyone for days and weeks at a time, read nothing, and listened to no music. I was able to practice living in the present moment full-time, with the grace of few distractions.

It became precious, this solitude. We need to enter the profound quiet of solitude before we can hear the voice of the soul clearly and in a sustained way.

When something emerges in our ordinary life that troubles us, that needs to be understood and integrated, we often fear it. So we turn to a friend or our therapist. We describe our conflict and look for comfort. We dissipate the energy that our experience had accumulated to teach us something. When we are alone we learn to listen to ourselves and take our own counsel. We come to trust ourselves, and then the lessons offered by our life emerge. We absorb their energy and move to new levels of understanding. We put ourselves in wisdom's way.

It is not necessary to go off alone for a long period of time. When we learn to follow our breath into our body and enter stillness, we can let solitude touch us in the midst of a busy life. We can find it while we commute to work, in meditation, in the bath.

FINDING THE BEASTS

To find the beasts we must enter the forest, walking into the darkest parts of our own shadow. It is the most frightening and exciting thing we can do. We go to meet all the things we have spent our life hiding from. We do not know who they are, what form they will take, or what we will encounter. It is the ultimate adventure, the archetype of all adventures. If we complete the adventure, we become master of our inner landscape. Nothing else need frighten us again.

Until we complete the adventure we cannot mature. Until the child, the victim, stands up within us and confronts what it is most afraid of, its fears will bind us. We will live in adult bodies, but our freedom will be no greater than that of a fearful child. Let us put aside the tyranny of the inner child and go to face the beasts. Let us turn around and confront what we have been running from all our lives.

As we begin our quest we know only two things. First, that we must meet the beasts on their own turf if we are to learn who we are from them. And second, that we have skills—a way of holding the mind stable and the heart open—that are equal to any challenge the darkest parts of our psyche can pose.

The portal into the forest is opened by a request to the soul. We must make it with absolute sincerity, with all the strength of our will, and with our whole body and mind, or else it will not work. The request is this: to be shown all that we are with nothing held back.

After we make this request, the portal opens in its own time. I made my request in my German atelier, once I knew that my prayers were being heard. I did not know what the journey would be like. I was wholly ignorant of what was going to happen. I had no way to know I was entering a process so painful, so riveting, and so completely rewarding.

I certainly had no way to know that the process, once begun, would unreel in a timeless quality beyond my control and that beasts would occupy all my energy, waking and sleeping, in dreams and visions, for six full months.

THE FIRST BEAST COMES

The first portal opened one afternoon as I was sitting in my room, meditating and enjoying the autumn sunshine as it poured through the window. I felt relaxed and at peace. I was thinking, "What could be more pleasant and serene? Perhaps this is what they mean by enlightenment."

My fatuity was the signal. Suddenly, my peace was shattered by intense pain in my heart. I had experienced nothing like it before. A fist had been shoved hard, right up through my diaphragm. I thought I was having a heart attack. And then the thought "Not a bad way to die" came, and I was surprised to find myself calm about death: "I'm meditating and at peace. Dying would be all right just now."

The pain went on, agonizing, and no death came. I was

willing to try anything because the pain was so unbearable, so I personalized it and talked to it. "You must be part of myself I've been avoiding," I said to it. What the hell was going on, and who was doing this to me?

I plowed on, whimpering, pleading: "I don't know who you are, but you obviously want my attention. You must be part of me. I give you my word right now that I will spend the rest of my life taking care of you, but first I need to know who you are. Come and take a walk with me. Tell me who you are and what you need. Then I will take care of you, no questions asked."

The pain began to diminish as soon as I had made my commitment. I was by now thinking of myself and the pain as "we." We went for a walk in the woods. Deep green almost marine light was drifting down. I asked my companion who it was. It was my anger. Not an experience of anger, or a set of angry feelings about someone. Anger itself, the compacted and buried anger of a lifetime, with memories of every occasion I had felt it.

Anger was the first of the beasts I met in the forests of my heart. It stayed for five days. During that time there was no getting away from it even for a second. We thought together, felt together, ate, slept, and dreamt together. I was shown things that changed my life. It was a showing, as Julian of Norwich, the great fourteenth-century Englishwoman and mystic, used that term. In intuition and thought, vision and dream, what I needed to see was given as a gift.

During that time, my life replayed like a movie. Again I thought of death. It felt like the stories one hears about someone's life flashing in front of his eyes. Only here the flashing went on for five days. Waking and sleeping, the movie played. It felt as different from my ordinary waking consciousness as a rain forest is different from a suburban garden. It had its own rhythm, its own duration. It was gentle, clear, not induced by any physical means or chemical substance. It felt designed for some specific purpose that I could not see, some teaching I could only wait to discover as it revealed itself.

I felt that I was being pushed to the limits of my abilities, both physical and mental. And yet there was no sense that I would have a bad ride, that I would be pushed beyond those limits. There was a great sense of intelligence and tender care behind the showing. The love that made the showing take place was as palpable as what was shown. I was being taught about myself in the way I had always hungered for.

I was shown all the relationships in which I had experienced anger and was given the chance to study the role anger had played in my life. I saw in detail how it had influenced each of the relationships in which it was present. While I worked as a lawyer, anger was a dominant color in the palette of my emotions. I discerned, too, the anger I had as a gay man in a culture that often condemned being gay. I observed the anger I had toward the Catholic Church, members of my family, people I worked with, myself.

Each of the relationships in which anger was key was seen in extraordinary detail all the way back to my earliest memories. The movie played relentlessly. Scenes were played and replayed, as I needed to study them. I felt but was not lost in the emotions that accompanied the images in every case.

Throughout this time, I remained in a clear awareness in which I could simultaneously relive my life and watch myself doing it with detachment and dispassion. It was this ability to watch that helped me see I was being given a gift of the soul.

The roots of the anger, when seen to the bottom, were always the same. I became angry because the world was not a better place. When I received pain from the actions of other people, I became angry. They should know better or be better. When church and government acted contrary to their stated purposes, I became angry. They should be more consistent, more honorable. When our society seemed to be heading into self-destruction, I became angry. We should not be this stupid.

After a couple of days I was forced to admit that anger was a far more dominant feeling in my life than I had believed. It was humiliating, and I resisted it. I had never thought that I had so much anger. It did not conform with the image I had of myself as someone who had worked on his life, had done psychotherapy, had specifically focused on anger. How was it possible to have so much anger and yet have a lot of friends, succeed in my work, and be enthusiastic about life?

In tears, I admitted that there was no longer any need to pretend to myself that I was other than who I was. It did not matter who I was. It only mattered that I could admit the truth as I had always longed to do.

Once I had owned the anger, I thought the movie would stop. Instead, I began to see how anger limited my freedom in all the situations in which it arose. Anger was a filter that I looked through to see the world, and I did not even know that it was there. When I was angry, I could not open my heart with the person I was angry with. I could not even open my mind.

Once it became clear how anger limited my freedom— and I had stopped grieving over how much of my life had been lost in anger—the showing moved toward its resolution. I saw that playing the victim had become a secret passion. I had become an adept of self-pity. I was convinced that I had reason to be angry with the church and society for condemning my gayness. And angry with colleagues, relatives, and friends for treating me badly. I was certain that these others had caused my anger, and as long as I believed that I could go on being a victim.

I wanted my freedom back, and could claim it only by laying aside the victim role forever and taking full responsibility before God for all the anger in my life. I would have to admit that every time I got angry it was because I chose to. Because

I *chose* to. Because *I* chose to. This was a mighty difficult thing to see. It directly challenged a central strategy of my life. For a whole day I tried to bargain with God. I said, "I'll take responsibility for all the anger in my life except the anger toward *him*. He's a real bastard, he hurt me, it's his fault, and I have good cause to be angry!" I offered a number of candidates for *him*.

I clung to my familiar suffering, my constitutional drama. Yet I knew I was at a crossroads. A point came after five days when I knew what I had to do. So I went walking in the country, following small lanes empty of cars, among green fields in which cows moved at their leisure. I needed to get out of rooms and walk under the open sky. I looked up, threw my arms wide open, addressed God, and said, "I'm finally ready to take absolute responsibility for all my anger throughout eternity."

At that moment, I felt a great shift within my being. I now had the freedom to choose any response that I wanted to use. This was real freedom, and it was mine, because I chose it. I had died to my former self and been reborn.

Anger still arises, and can catch me out. Now, though, I know that my freedom to choose is more fundamental than anger. It trumps it. I am the landscape, not the storm.

THE PROCESSION OF THE BEASTS

As my solitude deepened during my first six months in Germany, there was a series of visitations by one after another of the beasts in the forests of my heart. Each came in response to my call to know myself at last. Each was from a deeper and then a deeper shade of darkness. Each came only when I had met, come to know, and released the beast that came before it. After anger came despair, resignation, and sexual obsession, the passions that live in us and hold us in their thrall. Whereas anger had taken five days to release, despair and resignation each took several weeks. Sexual obsession took months.

Each of them was more difficult than the last to absorb. Anger was the one I knew best, so it came first. Despair I knew less well, and I was reluctant to admit it played as deep a role. I went to the root of it. The triple root of my despair was the pain I had taken within myself for being gay, my belief that humans were destroying the Earth, and my conviction that there was no God.

When resignation came on, I had to admit I did not believe I deserved a good life or to be happy, or that I would find love, human or divine. I did not believe that anything I could do would make a difference against the catastrophes I saw all around me. I was forced to admit that I had no vital emotional umbilical cord to anything that made life worth living. This was very painful to accept. How could I have such absolutely nihilistic feelings at the core of my life? And yet it was true. A radical hopelessness was eating away at my life, and I had not had the courage to see it.

I looked for sexual relationships as a way of finding some sanctuary of warmth and vitality because I had none within my own capacity to summon. I was looking to sexual relationships for what I could only find from within myself, and from a love affair with the Absolute.

In all, six months of full-time work, which was both exhausting and exhilarating.

The beasts that visit each of us may be different. What is always true is that until we release them, they enthrall us. We do not know this until each beast visits us in the sacred space we call forth by our absolute sincerity.

When I released anger, despair, resignation, and sexual obsession, they did not go forever. What changed fundamentally was my relationship to them. They had controlled my life and I was unaware of it. Now when they come, there is more room, more space to work. They still have lessons to teach, but now I have some of the objectivity I need to be able to learn from them.

For all their seeming ferocity, the beasts long for only one thing: to be set free. Their ferocity is the only way they know to get our attention. They will give us whatever painful experiences we need to become conscious of them. They do this because they can find release only with our conscious help.

REBUILDING THE FOUNDATIONS
OF THE PSYCHE

As each of these beasts comes forward and we encounter it, a pattern emerges. We start with denial. Then we put aside denial and admit the presence of the beast. Anger came with a fist in my heart, and its presence was real. It was in my body, and I had to take care of it. When I admitted it, I was able to see that it was part of myself that I had not loved and taken care of. When we see that the beast has a human face, and that the face is our own, the beast is freed.

When we free the beast, we gain access to what it was guarding. For in each case the beast embodies a deep structure of our consciousness that we have labored long and hard to build. We have made it foundational to our consciousness. It has passed out of the realm of the visible and sunk into the realm of the invisible, there to perform its task, to be the bulwark against experiences we found threatening.

Although these structures may have worked well in our youth, we no longer need their protection. Because they have passed into shadow and are no longer visible, we cannot see the impact they have on us and how they limit our freedom. We know the uncomfort we feel, the vague unease. We sense constriction and feel condemned to repeat neurotic patterns.

Once we have freed a beast, we see the structure, witness the function that it plays, and see how it forms our life. Then we are able to tear down the deepest and most inaccessible structures of our psyche. Until we do, they will cripple our freedom and keep generating neurosis. We can change our most fundamental patterns of behavior and rebuild them along lines that better suit our growth, thus releasing tremendous energy that was used by the beasts.

Many people would deny that we can rebuild our psyche in this way, but they are ignorant of the practice we are investigating here. I describe my own experience so you can see that fundamental growth and change are possible when we commit ourselves to them with absolute sincerity. If you try, you can experience this for yourself. You have the power to tear down the prisons in your unconscious. We build our prisons; we can tear them down. *Vive la Révolution!*

This work is the spiritual enterprise. Unless we do it, we can never experience our freedom, and we will always be divided against ourselves. Until we know our beasts, we can put whatever illuminations we gain in their hands without even knowing it. We can have openings and put them in service of our greed; we can have awakenings and put them in the service of our lust; we can know much of our internal landscape and put our knowledge in service of our narcissism. We can end this willful blindness only by desiring the true knowledge of who we are above all else and committing ourselves completely to the guidance of the soul.

It was appallingly difficult for me to admit to myself, even in a blessed solitude, that anger, despair, resignation, and sexual obsession were prime determinants of my own life. Even when I had the evidence in front of me, I went on denying the obvious conclusions for as long as I possibly could. We fear the truth, and yet the truth, as we are told, will set us free. And nothing else ever will.

What are we not admitting to ourselves? That is the ground where we must go to meet our beasts. Where do our stories of self-justification lie? They are a map to the lairs of

the beasts. Do we spin stories for ourselves about the sacredness of sex to justify lust as part of a spiritual path? If so, we
are kidding ourselves and refusing to look at the passions that
bind us. Do we come up with justifications about drinking,
gambling, rage, victimhood, distant parents, abuse, overworking, overeating, not using our talents, feeling miserable?
Wherever we are spinning cocoons of justification, that is
where our beasts are hiding.

Our minds will not agree to meet our beasts, for there are
no guarantees of safety. We can do it only by walking to the
edge of the ocean determined to find the true pearl, placing
ourselves in the hands of our soul and jumping in. It is a magnificent adventure. It is also the most pragmatic work we
could undertake. I try to capture that dynamic in this poem:

> No pain can fail
> to guide the way
>
> to that shifting precinct
> of deep and silent sacrifice
>
> in which we, alone,
> embrace and offer all,
>
> become the pain
> and its source and then
>
> the world, our heart,
> suddenly expands,
>
> another circle of our
> dominion restored.

Meeting Your Own Beasts

How do we enter into this kind of experience if we want to do it on our own?

We begin by invoking the power of the Divine, so that we may walk unharmed into all we fear. We then invite the beasts to come forward in their own time. We receive them as they come, learn from them, and when we have absorbed their teaching, we release them.

We prepare the ground by speaking directly to the Divine, asking to awaken into the true understanding of our life, to be shown everything we need to know, to understand everything we have been running from all our lives, and for the courage to receive all that we will be given.

When you do this practice, you must take the time it requires. Do not undertake it until you are ready to know who you are and are prepared to receive the consequences. When you are ready, seek solitude. Take several days if you can: time to quieten yourself, to feel the deep birth of the request in your heart, and to make the request. You can also make the request in just one day if you have to, but find at least a day and make it your own.

If you have access to a quiet and beautiful natural spot, far from the thrum of machines, that is best. Go there, and let

yourself sink into solitude before you make your request. If
you cannot go to such a spot, you can still make your request.
You can let the power of your sincerity create the solitude you
need, even in your room in the city. Your intention is the most
important thing. Let it be strong and clear and real.

INVOKING DIVINE HELP

When you are ready, call on the Divine and ask for awakening. Feel your intention to know who you are in your heart.
Then let yourself feel it rise up from your heart, through your
head, to the Divine. You might use words like these:

> *"Father and Mother, I come to You today with all the
> pain in my life to ask for awakening. Show me now the
> truth of who I really am. Help me face everything I
> have run from all my life. I am tired of running, tired
> of not knowing, tired of this small self.*
>
> *"Let me open completely to You. Let me live in
> You, through You, and for You in everything I do. I
> give You myself completely, now and forever. I hold
> nothing back.*
>
> *"I give You my life and all its pains and problems.
> They are Yours now. Show me how to take care of
> them. Show me everything I need to see so I can
> awaken fully and remember You always. And give me
> the courage to accept it, whatever it may be."*

INVOKING THE BEASTS

When you have offered yourself to the Divine and asked for
help, it is time to invite the beasts to come forward and teach
you. Remember that the beasts are parts of ourselves that we
have fragmented off. They come for our attention, to teach us

about ourselves, and because they want to walk into the light and we are the only doorway through which they can enter into it.

When you feel secure in your connection with the Divine and ready to invoke the beasts, take the following steps with absolute sincerity.

Follow your breath into your body. Be fully present. Feel your connection with the source of all being. Feel yourself nourished, protected, held.

Feel your soul, an embracing loving energy, surrounding your body. Feel your body held within the soul, as within an egg-shaped ball of light.

When you feel ready, address your beasts:

"All you parts of me that I have denied, I call you forward now. I offer you my love. Come now and teach me what I need to know. I promise I will take care of you for the rest of my life, no questions asked. I will do whatever you need. Come forward to me now, and let us awaken together."

When you have addressed your beasts, return to stillness. Follow the breath into the body. Remain fully present in the body. Do not expect anything to happen at once. Simply enjoy your inner stillness. You have already done a great thing and must now be patient.

Once we have invited the beasts forward, they will come. It may take time; the unconscious is somewhat thick and stubborn. Have no doubt, though, that they will come. One of them may come one night when you are feeling lonely, after you have had a few drinks. You may feel it as agitation and not know what to do about it.

Whenever a beast comes, it will get your attention by causing discomfort in your body, emotions, or mind. It does this not to harm but because it is the only way it knows to get your attention. We can recognize that a beast has come to visit by feeling a sharp discomfort. Then what? How do we talk to our beasts?

If a mood of agitation comes, or a depression, or you feel a fist in your diaphragm, take it for a walk. It is one of your beasts, eager to talk with you. Ask it what it has to teach you and what it needs from you. And then listen with every fiber of your being. If you listen to what it has to say it will teach you.

Do not be afraid to spend time with one of your beasts. I found it helpful to have a romantic dinner with my depression. I set a table for two, cooked a good dinner, lit candles, poured wine. My depression was my oldest familiar, and knew me well. It had things to say that no one else could tell me. Make sure the meal is a good one, for you are celebrating. Let your depression know that you have stopped playing hard to get. You are not running anymore. You will look it in the eyes, because you need to know its message. Then, as you eat and enjoy the food and wine, listen to what the depression has to tell you.

When a beast comes to visit, it may stay a while. Live with it, welcome it into your home. Its teachings are all about how to take care of yourself. At a certain point, when it has taught you everything it can, the beast will want to move on. You are its doorway to the light. It cannot pass until you take its teachings and then release it. When the time comes, release it consciously by offering it. By this time you will know its name. Assume for a moment that it is anger. When the time to release it comes:

> Let yourself feel your breath. Follow your breath into your body. Be fully present in your body.
>   Feel your anger in your body. Let it collect in your heart so that you can offer it. When you have collected

it in your heart, offer it, and let it move up from your
heart through your head to the Divine.
    "I offer you all the anger of my life. It is Yours now.
Teach me how to work with anger and take care of it
for the rest of my life."

A succession of beasts will visit. Each visit will teach you
about a different aspect of yourself. Welcome the beasts.
They are yourself. Take their teachings and release them, and
you will never have to run from anything again.

Offering Praise for What Is

Mystics do not denigrate this world of joy and suffering. Sensing life with the whole body, seeing neither good nor bad, they appreciate the life in every leaf, every piece of garbage, every smile, and every blow to the heart from someone they had taken as a friend. Seeing life, they praise it.

Can we let ourselves be truly open to the wonder of life and not just to its pain? There is no reason on Earth a person cannot be a mystic and a banker, a mystic and a waiter, a mystic and a mom, a mystic and an elementary school teacher or a policeman.

One of the best-kept secrets in the world is that mystics have more fun. How can we experiment with being a mystic in the marketplace? For a start, we can offer praise. Offering praise for all that is may be a foreign concept to us. We are taught to focus on how to get more than we have and not to be satisfied with what we do have. So strongly do we want to change things that we take little time to appreciate things as they are. Offering praise for all that is, is a strong action. It directly bypasses our critical faculties, ignores all our sophistication, and puts us in the position of accepting life as it is.

I came across the notion of praise as the highest form of prayer while reading Origen, who is one of my favorite heroes of the inscape. He was a brilliant mystic, theologian, and public speaker in the second century A.D. He believed in the reincarnation of souls and in a variety of other things not accepted by the later Church, which may be why he was never canonized. For a long time his notion of praise as the highest form of prayer puzzled me. I knew offering and asking. These seemed to me the forms of prayer that allowed our strongest emotions to move to the Divine. Praise seemed somehow artificial until I tried it. Praise and its afterimage, thanks, subtly change the tenor of the dialogue with the Divine. Their use moves the field of our expression beyond the sensations and needs of our own being to embrace the validity of all that is.

There is a Native American story in which the Creator gathers together in a great congregation all the beings on Earth. He tells them to stand in a circle near the others of their kind. What they must do, He tells them, is figure out their place, their job, their function, in Creation. What is their species meant to do? He tells them that when they have figured out their role in Creation, they are to come into the center of the vast circle and declare what it is.

So all the different species talk among themselves, and pretty quickly, some of them enter the circle. "We are to aerate and enrich the soil so that plants can grow more easily," the earthworms say. "We are to cull the old and sick of the deer and moose herds, so that the herds can be vigorous and of a size that balances the food supply," say the wolves. And so on, until everyone has spoken except for the human beings, who are standing on the outside, unable to resolve what their function in Creation is.

The other animals talk among themselves, seeing the embarrassing predicament of the humans, and send a delegation to speak to them. The leader, a badger, says to the human beings, "Why have you not spoken, like all the rest of us?"

And the humans say, one after the other, that they do not know their function.

"But we all know your function in Creation!" the badger says.

"What is it?" they ask all together.

"It's simple!" says the badger. "Your function is to praise all of Creation!"

There is another story of praise that I would like to share. It involves a friend who died of AIDS and the teaching he gave me before he died. I had been working as a volunteer with the Gay Men's Health Crisis in New York City in the mid-1980s, and was assigned to be what they called a crisis intervention worker for Tim, who was a man my own age, in his early thirties. He had moved to New York from North Carolina, where his father was a popular Christian minister, sadly full of condemnation for gay people. Tim had been in his twenties when he arrived in New York, and was thrilled to find a place where he could be himself at last. A talented musician, he played piano in clubs. Whenever he felt lonely or depressed, he went to the baths, where he felt accepted, acknowledged, and where he had a wild time.

When I met him, Tim was already very sick. Over the course of several months I went once a week to talk with him or to help with the things he could no longer do. I watched his body deteriorate rapidly from that of an attractive young man to that of an extremely elderly man. It was the intense chemotherapy treatments for his cancer that did it, along with the fact that his teeth just started falling out. I would find them on his nightstand.

Not long before his death I moved to the West Coast. As a farewell, he decided to take me to a chic new French restaurant in the West Village, a block and a half from his apartment. These were still the early days of AIDS. In the restaurant, I saw some people look at Tim, realize he was dying of AIDS, and then look at me, wondering if I was his lover and if I would be next. We had a good and celebratory dinner nonetheless, since Tim did not see pity and did not care about it.

As we walked back to his apartment, he had to stop frequently. He was walking with a cane, and his legs did not work very well. I was feeling pity for him. And although part of me felt close to Tim, I also found myself uncomfortable at being with him, aware that I could not just let him be who he was. I wished very strongly that things were different for him. I knew they could not be, and I also did not know what to do with my feelings.

Just before we got to his door, we were standing still on the sidewalk on Fourteenth Street near Eighth Avenue, while Tim rested. Suddenly he smiled a huge, gap-toothed smile and said to me, "I never realized until just now how every day is full of wonder!"

We parted, and I cried all the way home, walking across town to the East Village. I cried in relief, in pain, and in the knowledge that he had reached a level of understanding that transcended all the obvious pain in his life. I knew that he had given me a gift of praise, which was also a challenge. If he could see the wonder in every day, so could I see, and so could we all, no matter what our circumstances. The approach of death had clarified Tim's heart. The question he had given me was: why wait? Why not search for that clarity now?

As we offer praise, we acknowledge the wisdom of the patterns behind the reality that we can see and feel. By acknowledging that wisdom, particularly when we do not understand it, we bring ourselves into alignment with what is and with the source of what is.

How shall we practice praise? An eighty-four-year-old friend of mine recently told me that during times of unbearable physical pain, he repeats, "Holy, holy, holy, Lord God of Hosts, Heaven and Earth are filled with Your glory." This has allowed him, he said, to stand in what is fundamental while his senses are under the distorting influence of pain.

HOW TO OFFER PRAISE WHILE IN PAIN

Praise in moments of elation is being grateful for the best that we have. Praise in time of war within ourselves helps us remember the precious value of our life:

> *"For this very life, even while I am lost in pain, I praise You. For this experience of pain that has humbled my pride again, I praise You. For this life that runs on under all my difficulties, I praise You. For the sunlight on the grass on a September afternoon, I praise You. For all the unlikely beauty of the Earth that I will never see, I praise You. For my death, which will be no death, I praise You.*
>
> *"Help me to learn to praise, for my mind is often too clouded to know the shape of praise."*

Praise may often be nonverbal. It can be offered in a certain poise of awareness that appreciates but does not possess. It may be expressed in that moment after we hear the beat of a bird's wing upon the air, in admiration for the way our eyes run with tears when we chop onions, in our receptivity to the force of a mountain, in our tender exploration of the texture of our lover's skin, in the wonder that comes upon us when an unconscious pattern of behavior emerges into the light of contemplation, and in innumerable other ways.

Let me practice praise today, the day of the autumn equinox. The light in Santa Fe is lemony on the stands of purple asters wild in the field and on the drifts of mustard-gold chamisa. Though the hummingbirds are still here, yesterday they were chuffed against a morning chill, and soon they will fly home to Mexico. The season's first evening grosbeak has just arrived, looking like a temperate parrot, sartorially elegant in green and black trimmed with yellow and white. Today the nuthatch stood upside down, as it loves to do, and made its raucous call, a kind of tooting bark. The rabbit, whom I call Albrecht because he reminds me of the rabbit in Dürer's watercolor, yesterday dug out for himself a squirrel hole abandoned for a year, but was displaced by the erstwhile squirrel later in the day. To acknowledge all this familiar play is praise.

We can also send out praise on waves of music. There are endless discoveries to be made in the music of praise in every record store. Play it, sing it, let it run through your mind. My favorite song of praise right now is Monteverdi's "Let the Whole City Rejoice!" (*"Jubilate Tota Civitas"*). It has the clarity of the full Moon, the freshness of a summer thunderstorm, and the overbubbling warmth of first love. When you feel like singing, sing!

As we experience the act of giving praise, we discover that it is an offering of what is, with the will to wonder and a sense of gratitude. Let us enjoy experiments in praise, elaborating them endlessly.

Loving-kindness

There is a powerful traditional practice known as loving-kindness. It is particularly efficacious in opening the heart, helping us feel love toward ourselves, and softening hard feelings we hold toward another person.

Loving-kindness is a practice of sending blessings from our heart to ourselves and to others. It complements the practice of praise, and in a certain way is its reciprocal. When we offer praise, we return the love we feel for Creation to its source. In loving-kindness practice, we share the universal love that streams into us with the elements of Creation.

The fundamental practice is a simple one. It begins with focusing love on ourselves, and then moves out in a series of steps to focus love on someone we are close to, someone who is neutral, someone we have had trouble with, and eventually to all beings.

This is how to do it:

Relax as you sit, and take time to come into a gentle and focused awareness. Let your awareness move to your heart. Feel whatever is there. It may be warmth, and an energy that is open. The heart may be tight, and in need of relaxation. Whatever you feel there, just be

*aware of it. If you have no specific feeling that is all
right too.*

*When your mind has fallen silent, you are ready to
begin the practice. Find your own form of words, ones
you are comfortable with. Let them be something like
these:*

*"May I be happy, healthy, live in safety, and be
free."*

*Say them three times for yourself. Say them gently
and slowly. If any feelings arise, just notice them and let
them go. "May I be happy, healthy, live in safety, and
be free."*

*When you have sent yourself this blessing, let some-
one arise in your mind who has been a benefactor of
some kind. It may be a teacher, a financial supporter of
your work, or someone who has helped you in some
other way. Think of this person as you say, "May they
be happy, healthy, live in safety, and be free." Say the
blessing three times.*

*Then let your mind find a person you do not have
strong positive or negative feelings toward, someone
you are comfortably neutral toward. Think of this person as you say, "May they be happy, healthy, live in
safety, and be free." Again complete three rounds of
blessing.*

*Now find someone with whom you have had diffi-
culties long ago or have ones that are current today.
Send a blessing to this person. Even if you cannot feel
it wholeheartedly, at least acknowledge that this person
needs love like everyone else. If they have acted to hurt
you, it may be because love is far from them and they
need to open their heart. "Let them be happy, healthy,
live in safety, and be free." Again complete three
rounds of blessing.*

Then let your attention turn to all the beings in your

*nearby environment. All the animals and insects, all the
plants and microorganisms. All the people with all their
problems. "May they be happy, healthy, live in safety,
and be free." When you have completed three rounds,
expand the scope of the blessing to all beings on Earth,
and then to all beings in the Universe.*

This is a powerful practice. It uses blessing to heal our
own hearts. We do not do the practice thinking that our
blessing will prevent the suffering of other beings. We know
from the facts of life that this cannot be so. It is impossible for
us to remove the suffering of others in this way. What we can
do is change our own heart.

We spend so much of our time judging ourselves and others. When we do this practice, we adopt instead a loving disposition toward ourselves and others. This is a powerful
corrective. The practice is particularly valuable for changing
our feelings toward those we have had difficulties with. Often
difficulties arise in part because of some hardness on our side
of the transaction. The practice can help us dissolve this. A
common experience among those using the practice is that
they will meet someone they have been having trouble with
and find that the hard edge between them has softened.

At a minimum, the practice trains us to bless and not to
curse those who cause us difficulty. Curses can come quickly,
habitually, and unconsciously. They may seem small and
insignificant. Whenever we wish someone ill, however, that is
a curse. What good do curses do us?

During the day, thoughts enter our mind about people
who have hurt us. Be aware of them. Do not feed them
energy. Instead, offer the thoughts and then offer a blessing
for those who have hurt you: "May they be well." This slowly
begins to dry up our reservoirs of pain. If the negative feeling
is particularly strong, we can use a special blessing. It comes
from the rabbi in *Fiddler on the Roof.* When the rabbi was asked

to give a blessing for the czar, who was no friend to the Jews, he thought for a moment and said, "May God bless him and keep him far from us." Such a blessing is miles better than a curse.

I often use a shorthand form of the practice in which I send love to all the people I have had difficulties with in life, all my enemies. It is a good tonic for a dark morning or a dark moment.

There is a caution that comes with this practice. It does not depend on us whether all beings are happy, healthy, live in safety, and are free. We must be careful not to let ourselves think that we are the center of the Universe, on whom all blessings depend. This may sound like an easy problem to avoid, but it can be very subtle. If we have a strong desire to control things in the world—and we all do—it is easy to shift out of the aggressive and obvious desire to control the world by force into the subtler desire to control it through love. If we use the practice in that way, it will inflate our ego under the guise of love, a nasty business that we will spend a long time untangling. If instead we use it to align our heart with what is good for all beings, train our heart to wish no evil to anyone, even our enemies, and remember that blessings do not depend on us, then we use it well.

Ravished by Grace, Penetrated by Light

After six months of releasing the beasts, harmony returned to the forests of my heart. I realized I could walk anywhere in my inner landscape without fear. I became less interested in my own story. When our own drama starts to interest us less, we can go much deeper. In a lyric poem, Saint John of the Cross says that we can go out into the night and meet our soul's Lover only when our own house is stilled. His image is precise. While the beasts rampage in our psyche, there is no stillness in our house. What Saint John calls the "purgation of the dark night of the soul" must happen first. This is what we have called releasing the beasts. It is what brings our house to stillness.

Saint John, mystic and poet, is the quintessential Western follower of the way of the heart. His poem captures the hidden romance of this way and the longing of the soul for the Divine. More remarkably, he captures the physical as well as psychic wounding and ravishment we feel when we open to our soul, and our soul lets us taste its Source. Saint John wrote:

One dark night,
inflamed with love's desire,
oh fortunate adventure!
I went out unseen,
my house being now all stilled. . . .

On that glad night,
in secret, for no one saw me,
nor did I look at anything,
without other light or guide
than my burning heart. . . .

Upon my flowering breast,
that I kept for him alone,
he slept
and I caressed him
in the breeze from the fanning cedars.

As the breeze blew from the turret,
and I loosed his hair,
he wounded my neck
with his gentle hand
and suspended all my senses.

I abandoned and forgot myself
laying my face upon my lover;
everything ceased, and I went out from myself
leaving my cares
forgotten among the lilies.

Saint John was writing from experience, in terms as close
to literal as language allows. It is possible for each of us to
experience this. The soul waits patiently through innumerable
lifetimes until we ask to still our house and go out to meet our
Lover. The light is always there, just above our head. If we ask
with absolute sincerity, it will enter, but we should know that
the quality of our sincerity determines the degree to which we
receive the light.

As the soul comes forward, we begin to feel that it medi-
ates and reconciles the one and the many, unity and duality.
In our mind, there may be great conflict between unity and

duality. In our soul's experience, which it shares with us, there is no conflict.

The relationship of the soul to our life mirrors the relationship of the soul to its Source. As the soul comes forward, it permits our life to open to the Source. This is the experience of grace, and we can have it at any time. We need only let our aspiration rise and offer our whole life.

When we do this, a process unfolds with a wisdom and timing of its own. In the first stage, all the wounds in our psyche, the shadow material in our life, the beasts in the forests of our hearts, come forward. When we take the time and solitude to get to know them and offer them love, we can heal and release them, as described earlier.

We touch all the wounds in our psyche and offer them healing. The wounds take more than one touch to heal, but that first true touch changes everything. After that, we become less interested in our dramas. The dramas serve only to make our wounds surface again and again until we gain the poise to look at them, admit they are real, and offer them the healing balm of love. Love and not self-pity, for it is precisely self-pity that keeps the wounds open and unhealed. In self-pity we are the victim; in love, the healer.

When we begin to feel the light enter, we are surprised at how physical it is. It begins gently, as if a feather were tickling the crown of our head. When we try to grab at it with our awareness, it goes away. It is teasing, playful, not to be caught. Once we have felt this contact, we want much more.

As our familiarity with the light grows, we begin to feel it as a Presence, initiating contact, responding to us, in every way as present as any person in a room with us and just as real. We feel and hear movements in the sutures in our skull, the junctures where bony plates have grown together. In a baby the bony plates have not yet grown together, and as we feel ours move, we feel again like a baby, being born into a new realm of experience.

There may also be sharp stabs, which feel like intense penetrations of the light down into our skull. This may be startling but is a sweet pain. Far from being frightening, it is encouraging: we feel the presence of a powerful force working to introduce itself into our life and our being in a real, pragmatic, physical as well as spiritual way.

As our skull is re-formed, we feel the barrier breaking down between the physical and the spiritual, and realize that both are part of a continuum. As the light enters our physical body, we feel that matter is only light in a dense form. We know with certainty that we are being made ready to receive more light. And more again, so that to embody it is all we yearn to do.

After the crown has been opened, we feel what seems like a great drop of water over our head, and it breaks, and pours into us. After this experience, we begin to be able to be more aware of the light, and feel it touch our head when we turn our attention to it.

This experience is captured in Christian iconography in the image of the Holy Spirit above the heads of the Apostles. As our experience teaches us, the Spirit is not ethereal, not a metaphor. The depiction of it entering the Apostles on Pentecost is an accurate one. As we do this practice, we may experience this for ourselves, in our own lives, in our own bodies.

This is grace entering and changing us. As we continue to long for the Presence, the Lover comes and fills us. Gradually, the light works its way down from the crown to the third eye, in the middle of the forehead. It then fills the entire head. Each stage of this progress is a miraculous, secret joy.

Over the course of months, the light moves from our head into the throat. We realize that this exquisitely precise unfolding comes from an astonishing and intimate Intelligence.

The light moves down into the heart. We are able to feel

what the mystical traditions call the subtle energy center of the heart and experience it as more real than our physical heart, which we have never felt with such precision. As the light enters our heart, we feel it first as a stabbing pain, as the light breaks down the armor we have built up around it.

We are astonished that this is happening in the realm of the physical, not the psychological. We may wonder if we are having a heart attack as this happens, but again know that we are being held, protected, taken care of.

We feel the heart dilate, open, and fill with a light of infinite sweetness. We want nothing else but to be with our Lover. When the heart opens like this, our third eye and crown are open too, all full of blissful energy. This is what we have always longed for and needed without knowing it.

The light continues to penetrate farther and farther down into our physical system. We feel it in each of our subtle energy centers, all the way to the base of the spine. As the light establishes itself there, it refines our sexual longings and experience. We begin to value sex as the expression of love, as the physical ground in which intimacy can deepen.

We may have the experience of a snakelike energy uncoiling and rising from the base of the spine up and out through the crown. The Indian yogas call this experience the kundalini rising. Although it is a powerful experience, it is a small thing compared to the force of the light opening us, seeking to enter ever more deeply into the material realm through the vehicle of our bodies.

This feeling of the light coming down is a direct experience of the soul entering into the material realm through us. Progressively, we come to accept the soul's presence, call it to us, and release our troubles into its serenity, vast as space. Grace can come unbidden. It also comes when we call it. It waits with infinite patience. We need only ask with our whole heart.

6

The Way
of Action

Introducing the Way

The ways of heart and mind strip away our false conceptions about ourselves. We gain clarity of mind and heart to act freely in the world for the good of others. Practice makes of our pain a doorway; emerging on the other side, we can see into other people's pain and find a measure of compassion.

Though the ways of mind and heart require stillness, they do not make us hermits. Perhaps at an earlier stage in human culture, those who enjoyed these ways could do so in continuous solitude. For most of us, except for periods of deep stillness in which we explore and refresh ourselves, solitude is not the answer. Engagement is. An engagement in which we work in whatever capacity we can to help others and to help the Earth.

We are what we do. All the awakenings in the world mean nothing if we are not loving in our actions. Do we take care of our own life and all the life around us? To do so is the way of action.

If we try to do good without taking care of our own needs for clarity, we may do some good, but we will exhaust ourselves. We will often fight ourselves without knowing it. Or find ways to lose, so as to confirm our own secret, negative feelings about ourselves.

Advice from the Dalai Lama

Midway through my time in Germany, my life became reduced to a knife-edged question: How can I bring spiritual and environmental practice together? I traveled to Dharamsala, India, in the foothills of the Himalayas, to ask the Dalai Lama this question. Through the good offices of a friend, a private audience with His Holiness was arranged. We spoke in his study for well over an hour. I told him my question. His advice was clear.

"You must become confident and positive," he said. "And then you must help others to become confident and positive. The long-term solutions we need to world problems, including environmental problems, can never emerge out of an angry mind."

I returned to Germany and studied his answer. Having met and released the beast of anger before my trip to Dharamsala, I was ready to understand his point of view in a way I would not have been before. Anger, he was saying, is incompatible with long-term creative vision. Such breakthroughs come from minds more open than anger allows. Even subtle anger—repressed and unvoiced, possessing us with no visible signs—blocks such positive breakthroughs.

My work as an environmental lawyer had been mostly fueled by anger, which took a high personal toll. What was less obvious was that because I worked from anger I was unable to put aside the aim of beating my opponents long enough to come up with a positive vision. What was I working toward, beyond the next federal case, the next congressional elections, the next attack from antienvironmental interests? I did not really know.

I have been surprised to find how widespread this lack of vision is among top environmental leaders, and how common the relationship between it and anger. Before I returned from my long retreat in Germany, I had completed the first part of the assignment the Dalai Lama had given me. I had become confident and positive. To begin the second part, I wanted to see how other environmental leaders felt.

I got a grant from the Nathan Cummings Foundation and spent several months talking to top American environmental activists, some seventy-five people in all. We talked about their relationship to their work, their day-to-day motivation, and about resources they could turn to for self-renewal and for developing a positive vision. What they said troubled me. Almost every one of these professional activists, lawyers, scientists, lobbyists, the top environmentalists in the country, told me the same story. It ran roughly this way:

> My work is based on anger. What we are doing to the Earth upsets me deeply. Because it makes me angry, I work for change. But I am convinced that all the policies we all advocate will not make enough of a change. We need a much bigger and more fundamental change. None of us sees what needs to happen or how to get to the answer. Not the experts, not the grass roots, certainly not the politicians. I don't know any way to find a compelling positive vision, so I keep working from anger. I know it's not enough and will burn me out, but I have no other source of fuel and would collapse without it. When it comes to support-

ive structures, the religion of my youth has no power
to help me, and I do not know where else to turn.

It was not the story itself I found troubling, for I had felt
the same way before my long retreat. What was disturbing
was the impact of hearing the same story again and again
from all the most dedicated and brightest—the layer upon
layer of fatigue, anger, and lack of vision. Nor do I think that
any other mainstream group in our culture has a more positive
vision than the environmentalists have.

If we can learn to use the energy of anger skillfully, it can
become a powerful weapon in our arsenal. Used well, it can
give us the energy to fight the battles we need to win. Anger
alone, though, cannot be our main companion through every
working day. It wears us out and shuts us down.

The ways of the mind and heart take us beyond anger.
They let us experience the healing that comes from connect-
ing to the source of our being. They therefore make us confident and positive. They let us walk anywhere in the inscape
with freedom and without fear.

How do we take this knowledge beyond our personal
experience? How can we act confidently in the world from a
place beyond anger? Let us begin by asking two questions.
First: What do we need from the world? And second: What
does the world need from us? Once we know these things, we
will ask another question: How do we find a radical confidence that stands up to experience in a world that often seems
to be spinning into chaos?

What We Need from the World

When we look on the world around us, we see a great deal that needs changing and we naturally want to bring about that change. But we quickly run into a paradox: when we want to change the world, we tend to link our own happiness to it, and in so doing we create suffering for ourselves.

Let us look again into the difference between pain and suffering. Pain enters the life of every human being, from the pain of giving birth and being born to the pain of growing old. There is often little we can do about it. If I have a toothache, it hurts no matter what my practice is. Suffering is something we add to pain. Whereas pain is a fact about being embodied in the world, suffering is a torture we manufacture for ourselves by holding on to our pain, insisting the world change so as to erase our pain, and making our happiness dependent on it. We are master craftsmen at suffering. We are connoisseurs of it and, when we gossip, raconteurs of it, too.

A familiar example comes from romantic love. If a lover leaves us, we experience pain, which may come in the form of grief, anger, or fear. We want the world to be different: we want our lover back and refuse to be happy without him or her even though we may know that the other person is incapable of loving us and we are better off alone. Our suffering is immune to facts precisely because it is generated by wanting the world to be different.

If we want to cut off suffering, we must stick to the facts. Pain has a natural periodicity, a waveform. We can become aware of it, like a piano tuner is aware of the rolling pulse that defines a note as an A. When we know the waveform of the pain, we can ride it back to its source. When we reach the source, we can touch it with the healing balm of awareness, and the pain will diminish in its own time. But when we use memory to prolong the pain and relive it, refreshing and refeeling it, we create suffering. We may let the refreshed memory of our pain carry us on to the memory of other pains inscribed within us. Drawing suffering like threads out of the refreshed memory of pain, we weave a tapestry of suffering for ourselves.

As long as we want the world to change to suit us, and make our happiness contingent upon such change, we will suffer. Is a healthier environment or the abolition of world hunger a precondition of our happiness? Our suffering will not help the environment or feed the hungry. If we refuse to be happy until the world is different, we are simply refusing to be happy. We are also, perhaps, not being fully honest with ourselves. We can easily use the problems of the world as a screen to hide behind.

So the paradox is this: we want the world to change; but for our own psychic health we must not be attached to the change taking place. It may seem a subtle point. Within it, however, lies a key to acting freely and to ending much of our suffering.

What do we really need from the world? Not very much, when we look into it. Certainly not in the way of wealth, possessions, celebrity. Samuel Beckett said that the thirty years of his adult life lived in obscurity were the happiest times of his life.

Each of us needs to answer this question for himself or herself. Take a moment and do it:

Relax into your breath and follow it into your body. Allow your mind to go quiet.

In stillness, ask yourself, "What do I really need from the world to fulfill my human life?"

My answer is: simple food, clothing, and housing; a few people to love; some quiet communion with Nature; work that challenges my talents; medical help when needed; and some money to interact with the world. The rest is extra. Those extras, of course, can be delightful. I love drinking wine and tasting within it the soil the grapes grew in. I love honey gathered as nectar by ten thousand bees from flowering oak and chestnut and high mountain flowers. I love the happy mammal feeling of a delicious meal in a beautiful place with a loved one, and what comes after it. The excitement of travel just when I feel the need for it. A fine concert in a foreign land serendipitously chanced upon. And innumerable other things. The myriad pleasures of life, though, taste sweeter and cleaner when we do not need them. Need removes the clarity from enjoyment.

We think we need all manner of things: more money, friends with better connections, greater success in our career, enlightenment. We work terribly hard for these things. While we are doing this, are we enjoying our life? If not, what are we working for?

I like the story of Diocletian and what he needed from the world. Diocletian was a Roman emperor who ruled during a difficult period. The empire was at the height of its territorial expansion but no longer at the height of its powers. Highly competent, dedicated, and an administrator of some genius, Diocletian ruled innovatively and well, and for a while he stabilized the empire's decline. There were a few other Roman emperors who managed this during their reigns. Diocletian went beyond these: in the midst of his reign he resigned, retired to an estate far from Rome, and gave up public life completely. He then enjoyed his quiet. He must have had unusual clarity about what he needed from the world.

His retirement was not understood in Rome, although he had tried to prepare people for it, and there were many attempts to interest him again in the affairs of state. Why would a man walk away from being the most powerful man in the world to live in the country? Diocletian wrote to a former colleague to explain.

"If only," he wrote, "they could see in Rome these cabbages I grow with my own hands!"

Few men have ruled the world and retired early to raise cabbages. Few could give up absolute power and limitless wealth, but Diocletian did. He must have been comfortable with himself. Few of us can sit quietly with ourselves even for an hour. Most of us are almost always hiding from ourselves in noise, drama, and busyness. Diocletian could have kept running from himself and received only praise for it, as we do for overworking and being overcommitted. We gain in self-importance from these things. Diocletian saw that they were empty. When we can be quiet with ourselves, we can see what we need from the world. Aside from a few simple things, nothing.

My partner, Martin, and I have been conducting an experiment in simple living for the past few months now. We have been living in an ancient Cathar village in the Pyrenees in the south of France. We have no car, no TV, no stereo, no heat. A telephone, but no one to call. No way to avoid being quiet. Time to find the orchids blooming among the thyme and lavender, poppies and irises, pomegranates and figs. Time to find out how alive these hills are although people have lived in them for almost half a million years.

We have time to watch eagles and golden orioles. To get to know the daily rhythms of the cinnamon-colored falcon and listen to the nightingales. Time to rescue frogs and snakes and salamanders from the irrigation canal. Time to feel the sequential birth of living beings in a landscape as the cold rains of winter end, spring opens itself out, and then everything pulses into summer. Time to focus on love for one's partner, the Divine, and oneself, three sides of an eternal triangle, supported by the natural world. Time to write and to gather one's deepest purposes before venturing into the world again. Once we know how to be quiet with ourselves, many of the things we thought we needed are revealed to be distractions.

What the World Needs from Us

We all think we are special. We think this because we are identified with our drama rather than with our soul's perspective. We long to have a shining place in the ecosystem of communal attention, a niche in which to be admired. We fear we do not exist if we do not get this attention every little while.

Because we think we are special, we believe that the world needs us. When we devote our life to doing good in some way, we are particularly susceptible to this belief. We may think we have a crucial mission to fulfill in making the world a better place. This is arrogant nonsense and nothing more. If any one of us, no matter how special we feel, were to die tomorrow, the world would survive. The world needs none of us. If you find this jarring, stop and work your way through it. If it troubles you, do not leave it alone until you make your peace with it.

Our families do not need us. Our friends do not need us. Our role in life does not need us. History does not need us. When we die, adjustments will be made and life will go on. There may be grieving and hardship, but life will continue. What a relief it is to know this. If we think we have a special mission in the world, we carry a heavy burden. For a long time I thought this way. I saw that environmental problems were overwhelming and that few people devoted themselves to solving them. I believed I had both the right intentions and the necessary skills. I convinced myself of the importance of my role. Or perhaps *convinced* is too strong a word. It did not take much of an argument because I was eager to believe it. The fact that it was an illusion made the burden no lighter.

If you have to save the world, you are also not much fun. A former colleague turned down an invitation to lunch by saying, "I don't have time for lunch; I'm saving the ozone layer!" Lunch went on without him and was certainly jollier. That is no small thing.

Giving Up the Fruits of Our Actions

When we absorb that the world does not need us, we can begin to sense a related truth: the world is already fine as it is. We focus so intently on what is wrong that we miss the fundamental perfection of things. We may catch it in moments, and then lose it again as we focus on problems. From the soul's vantage, the fundamental perfection of the world and what needs changing are simultaneously seen. When we accept the possibility that both sides of a paradox are true, we make an opening that invites wisdom in.

We already know this breadth of vision that embraces paradox on a more intimate scale. When we love someone in a way that leads us to accept everything about them, we see two aspects. We see their fundamental perfection, but also what causes them suffering—and what, were it to change, would cause them less suffering.

Life on Earth is the life of Gaia, which has been living itself for billions of years and will go on doing so for billions more. There is perfection in it. When we can see the inherent perfection of things, and recall that it is our insistence on changing the world that makes us suffer, a power arises within us. It is a power of releasing and letting go.

Freedom in action comes from releasing the fruits of our action. We still act to effect an outcome, because that is the only way we can act, but we release the internal demand that the outcome emerge as we have envisioned it. This internal insistence adds nothing to the success of our action and guarantees that we will suffer if we do not succeed. Relinquishing this requirement makes us less dependent on success.

There is a developmental way in which success is important, of course. If we failed in everything, we would feel permanently adrift. As we experience success we fashion an ego that lets us navigate the world confidently. We need to fashion such an ego before we can mature, for until we do we have nothing to transcend. After all, Diocletian was able to renounce the imperial throne because he sat on it. It is when the hand of success opens that it sows the seeds of detachment.

We also need some failure. Failure is a signal event in the most original lives. Both Freud and Gandhi, for example, suffered deep failures after their early successes. They withdrew as they entered their middle years and fashioned the work we remember them for. Failure can move us to call from the implicate order the solutions to our deepest problems.

Once we have tasted both success and failure innumerable times, we can move beyond them both. When we see both of them as stepping-stones to maturity, we open to the wisdom of releasing the fruits and enjoying the work.

ASKING THE SOUL TO DO THE WORK

We can ask the soul to come forward, move through us, and accomplish the work we need to do in every detail. It does not matter how insignificant the work seems; we can ask that which is greater to use us and accomplish it.

When we do this, surprising things begin to happen. If we are doing creative work, we feel our creativity increase measurably. If we are experiencing writer's block, it will untie the knots. If we are nervous about speaking in public, asking in this way will allow the words to flow on their own. A manual task is a good time to feel this, since we can let our mind fall silent and enjoy the flow of our body and the work. Every one of our actions is already being effected by our true self; we can know this for ourselves if we only open to it.

When we are exhausted but need to keep going, asking the soul to come forward and take over will produce the energy we need to fulfill our responsibilities. When we ask to have the work done through us, we begin to feel somewhat detached from the work, and we feel the soul's spaciousness around it. We begin to enjoy it more. When Mozart gave a particularly good performance, he would write to his father that it "went like oil." As we ask to have the work done through us, it begins to go more easily and with no worry.

WHY ACT?

The way of action may begin to sound like a counsel of lethargy. If the world does not need our action, and if we are not attached to outcomes, why act at all?

We act to make sense of our own life and to enjoy our talents in their growth, development, and full and free play. We prefer to work toward a good end, rather than lapse into accidie, whether or not our action succeeds. We spontaneously want to care for people and the Earth, because to relieve the pain of others comes naturally to us. We act because it is more fun.

WHAT ABOUT AMBITION?

What happens to ambition in the way of action? Do we hang it up on the wall?

Absolutely not. World-beating ambition is consistent with this path and is a projection of our will into the world. Without ambition we are ineffectual, and this is a kind of living death. Mother Teresa and the Buddha were as ambitious as Napoleon and John D. Rockefeller. The question is this: What are we ambitious for? To satisfy our selfish interests alone? Or on behalf of the good? We may conceive of the good in many ways, all of which are superior to our private advancement.

When we are ambitious on behalf of the good something extraordinary happens. We start becoming selfish on behalf of others. We become selfish for those we see in needless pain and want to help them. We become selfish for the Earth and want to help it too. Our impulses on behalf of others motivate action far beyond the purview of our own small selves.

DOING THE POSITIVE

How do we release the fruits of our action and know in our bodies that the action is being taken not by but through us? The practice runs counter to a lifetime of experience and to the expectations of our culture. Once again recall: it is not how often we forget but how often we remember that counts.

The elements of the practice are simple. When we begin any action, we dedicate it and ask that it be done through us. Every action big or small, at work and at home:

"I offer this action and its results to You. Please do the work through me now, and let me feel You do it."

Then, as we do the work, we keep returning to the present moment, back to the body, back to the breath.

So as we sit in a meeting, we return constantly to the body and to the breath. There is all the time in the world to be present in the meeting, make our points, and return to the body and breath.

As we stand in a courtroom or a classroom we do the same thing. As we peel an onion or wash the dishes. As we help someone in a hospital bed. As we sit down to our computer terminal. As we clean up after the children. As we balance the checkbook and take out the garbage.

We also begin to notice when we are eager to claim credit: "I did this!" We offer this feeling when we find it. We begin to find ourselves happy when others take credit for our ideas. What makes them ours, after all?

When our actions fail, we offer the failure and all our associated feelings. If our feelings are too confused for us to name them clearly, we offer the confusion. When our action succeeds, we offer that, and remember that we only contributed our talents to the action and that our talents are not ours in the first place.

AVOIDING FANATICISM

The world is full of fundamentalists and religious fanatics, more so all the time. What is to keep us from following the ways of mind, heart, and action, only to turn into fanatics, brownshirts eager to impose our views on others?

The path of ensouled action itself weeds out our innate tendencies to fanaticism. A fanatic believes he knows the truth and has the right to impose it on everyone else by any means. The fanatic is obsessed by outcomes. If he tells you of his god and you disagree, he may be moved to kill you.

The greatest temptation on the path is to believe we embody the truth so fully that whatever actions we take express it. When we believe this, we can justify anything we do—seduction, betrayal, murder, all seem justifiable.

If we forget that our understandings are always partial, that for every awakening there will follow a deeper awakening, we suffer a madness that takes many forms: some call themselves prophets, ambassadors, or messengers of the Divine; others call themselves perfect masters, gurus, or führers. Such people have had a powerful inner experience of some kind. They have failed, however, to take the experience into their life, integrate it, and use it as a point of leverage to do the slow, patient work of transforming their conduct. Instead, they became dazzled by their experience, let themselves be unbalanced by it, and seek to dazzle others.

It is hard, patient work to move on from visions and awakenings to this integration into ordinary life. It is far more glamorous to become a divine messenger, but to think we are special in this way is to choose a kind of insanity.

When we have an awakening, we have the chance to go back to our life and to bring all our habits into the light of the awakening, until we transform them. This is the heart of our practice. When we stop obsessing about ends and concentrate on means, we begin to penetrate the relationship between ends and means and become less interested in trying to compel others to share our point of view.

Radical Confidence

We have seen how to transform our anger and fear and all the other feelings that afflict us. Yet it is not only the character of our experience that needs changing but the nature of our culture. We begin by working with our own experience. How can we move outward and translate the confidence gained in our inner work into a positive view of the world?

Let us begin by looking at the mind we all share, what might be called the consensus mind. It is a structure of ideas, norms, and beliefs, tacitly held, that shape the experience of being in our society. Much of what we think of as our own ideas about the world, who we are, and what is worth striving for is taken in from our culture. What we think of as private mental space is occupied by these culturally produced and distributed notions. This shared and overlapping structure is what we will call the consensus mind. Unfortunately, much of it is maladaptive.

The consensus mind is certainly no more enlightened than our own. Just as our own neurotic structures block us, the same is true for the consensus mind. It suffers the traumas of war, famine, plague, and all the rest, and is deeply affected by these. It develops a set of patterns of thought and feeling every bit as tight as our own, and its vision is constricted by them in the same way as our own. Much of our difficulty in communal life as families and as nation-states is born of the fact that we are blinded by our consensus ideas.

It is easy for us to see how anger, despair, and greed contribute to our personal unhappiness. What structures in the consensus mind are homologous to these, and so have a structure and function in the consensus mind parallel to them? To find a neurotic idea in the consensus mind, we need to look at what is taken for granted, hallowed, and untouchable. What is the most sensitive area for people who have built their lives around being victims? What will they react most violently against? It is simple: the notion that they can be strong, responsible for their own feelings, and happy.

Where is a parallel in the consensus mind? I would suggest that the notion of boundless economic growth is one of these. As a society we hold on to the idea of growth with the kind of unreflective tenacity that marks the presence of a neurotic structure. We do not have open debate about what growth means, how it can be infinite in a world of limited resources, who are the beneficiaries and who the losers in growth as we pursue it, or how we count destruction of natural resources against growth. We do not discuss as a people what the long-term implications are of adhering to indiscriminate growth as a central social dogma.

Just as one who has created a persona around being a victim reacts angrily when told that there are other perspectives, the consensus mind reacts angrily when its devotion to growth is challenged. This makes it difficult for any individual to look into the notion. If we do, and understand its implications, we are at first daunted. We see that we as a culture are very likely headed for disaster unless we change our views and learn to discriminate within our devotion to growth. Seeing this, we feel alien from and critical of our society.

We see that our culture has been dedicated to a self-destructive approach and that we must live with the consequences. In an earlier time, the notion of boundless growth was adaptive. Evolution favored those who had as many children and consumed as many of the Earth's resources as possible, just as it favors any species that does these things. Economic growth as we hold on to it is a consensus memory of this earlier time.

It is no longer a good idea to consume as many resources as quickly as we can, but our attachment to the notion has passed below consciousness. We justify decisions that tear communities and families apart, move jobs offshore, increase the disparity between rich and poor, and destroy precious natural resources, all in the name of economic growth, without ever questioning the basic premise. This consensus behavior runs parallel to the way in which we develop individual neuroses; a behavior that may have been adaptive long ago is retained, calcifies, passes out of consciousness, and now prevents our adaptation to new circumstance. The seeds of liberation and confidence lie within this arresting realization.

It becomes possible to see that economic growth is a set of ideas, attitudes, and behaviors in the consensus mind. Deeply rooted as it is, it is no different from maladaptive patterns in the individual mind. Moreover, the consensus mind is no other than our mind.

We reify the consensus mind and the ideas at play in it, and grant them a permanence and a concreteness that they do not have. Once we repeatedly transform anger and despair in our individual experience, confidence can emerge about the consensus mind as well. When we change our own minds, we take a step toward changing the consensus mind.

CHANGING THE WORLD
ONE MIND AT A TIME

Let us do an exercise in which we explore our relationship to economic growth and look into the evolution of patterns in the consensus mind.

Follow your breath into your body. Become fully aware
of the breath, fully aware of the body. Let your mind
enter silence.

Then, begin to investigate your relationship with
the notion of economic growth. What does economic
growth mean to you? Take some time to look into this
question.

Do you need the new car, new appliances, new
home, and all the rest that spur growth?

What will make you happier: working an extra
twenty hours a week to pay for a new car or spending
those twenty hours a week with your family, biking,
gardening, writing poetry, or whatever you most love to
do?

Which do you prefer: fancier possessions or a
deeper appreciation of the miracle of life itself?

Once you have satisfied your own basic needs and
those of your family, what would you most like to do
with your precious human life?

What are you here to accomplish?

What is your life for?

Take time to sit with these questions in silence.
Stay with them until some aspect of an answer comes.
Then keep the question with you and, holding it open,
use it as a benchmark to test everything you spend
time on.

When we give up an attachment to boundless economic
growth in our own life, we have an impact on the consensus
mind. As others also give up the idea, it has less vitality and
ultimately expires. This may seem hard to envisage. But consider: within human history, we have given up the idea that
cannibalism is appropriate; within the last century and a half,
we have given up the idea that slavery is appropriate; within
the last couple of decades, the rights of women and gay peo-

ple have started to be taken seriously; within the last few years, sexual abuse has been brought into the open.

Each of these is a deep, evolutionary change that has taken place because enough individuals made a transition within themselves to a better form of thought. When enough individuals make such a transition, there is a phase change in the consensus mind.

It may nevertheless be difficult to conform social behavior to changes in the consensus mind. The American Civil War is an extreme example of this difficulty. Even there, however, slavery had to end once the idea of universal freedom was widely shared. We can transform our own minds. By seeing into the roots of our maladaptive behavior and weeding it out, we gain a fuller access to the free flow of life. We can, therefore, also transform the character of our culture, since it is composed of the individual experience of each of us.

When we see this, we gain the perspective of radical confidence. Not only can we walk the inscape unafraid, we can walk the outscape unafraid. Transformation in both inscape and outscape may be difficult; it may be long-term; but it is possible.

This is not naive idealism. The mere publication of a better notion than boundless growth will not change the facts of life, any more than merely hearing that it is possible to transform anger changes our experience of it. But hearing that there is a way out of anger is a beginning of the way out. The same is true of growth or any other idea in the consensus mind.

Despair counsels that the game is already over. Radical confidence says it has only just begun. We can act meaningfully for change and create a society more caring of its members and in harmony with the Earth. With the personal experience of transformation and the assurance it affords, we can move forward with the myriad patient acts of that creation. We can focus on those acts and let the outcome be revealed in trust.

There is a story that illustrates nicely the value of letting go of the fruits of our actions. A saint is walking along a road. He is obviously a saint, since he is beatific and shining with light. He passes a beggar on the road, and the beggar asks him where he is going. The saint replies that he is making a periodic visit to the Divine, to give a report on his work in the world.

The beggar asks the saint if he will ask the Divine how long it will be until he is enlightened. The saint says yes and continues on his way until he comes to a well-dressed monk sitting under a tree in meditation. The monk asks the saint where he is going. When the saint replies, the monk too asks the saint to ask the Divine how long he must wait for enlightenment.

Some time later, the saint is coming back along the road. He sees the monk. The monk says, "Did you ask the Divine how long it will be until I am enlightened?" "Yes," says the saint. "I'm afraid you will have to wait two more lifetimes until you gain complete enlightenment." "Two more lifetimes!" says the monk. "That's terrible, and me here practicing and practicing as hard as I possibly can!" The saint bids him good-bye and keeps walking.

Eventually he comes to the beggar. The beggar says, "And did you ask the Divine how long it will be until I am enlightened?" "Yes, I did," says the saint, looking sad. He points to a nearby tree, tall and full of leaves. "I am sorry," he says, "but you will have to suffer as many more rebirths as a beggar as there are leaves on this tree before you are enlightened." With that the beggar stands up, claps his hands, and dances. "Imagine that!" he exclaims. "Only a little while until I meet my Lord!" And with that he was perfectly enlightened.

Balancing the Three Ways

In the ways of mind, heart, and action, we invite the soul to come forward. As the soul comes forward into the mind, we experience the mind ensouled; as it comes forward into the heart, we experience the heart ensouled; and as it comes forward in our action, we experience ensouled action.

One and then another of these paths may appeal to us at different times in our lives. Experiment, and trust your intuition. Combining elements of each over time is a way to balance. We can get unbalanced by following a single way.

When we practice the way of the mind alone we may become a little grim. The way of the heart melts grimness. When we practice the way of the heart alone, we may have visions and ecstasies but find no way to integrate them into our lives. The way of the mind allows us to see that visions and ecstasies are not important in themselves. They have value only insofar as they encourage us into deeper understanding. The way of action brings our practice directly into our work in the world and into all our work relationships. It helps us remember that our practice is not confined to our times of silence but flows over into our whole day.

We may become confused when we shift between the ways of mind and heart. After all, the way of the heart relies on devotion, and the way of the mind on a type of analysis.

We may have a schizoid feeling as we move from one to the other. We can resolve this by exploring both and accepting each as ultimate.

We are familiar with the notion in physics that light has a dual aspect. It will behave either as a wave or as a particle, depending on the intention of the observer. It is not that light is waves or particles; it is experienced, irreducibly, as both.

So it is with our perception of the ultimate. Our mind will see the wavelike properties of thought and feeling. It will see experience as waves arising from the ocean of being and falling back again. For the mind, there is only vast spaciousness, with transitory phenomena. Not so the heart. Where the mind sees waves, the heart personalizes. The heart encounters beings. Its natural mode is to be in relationship. Devotion to an entity greater than ourselves therefore arises spontaneously.

Just as light has a wave-particle duality, our experience of the ultimate has a wave-entity duality. It is not reducible, any more than light is reducible. Which we perceive will depend upon our intentions and our practice. In the end, the paths merge. If we follow the way of the mind to the end, the heart will open. If we follow the way of the heart to the end, the mind will open. If we follow the way of action to the end, mind and heart will also open. All three are real. Each has its own rhythms, its own trials, its own revelations.

In the end, we need all three ways. As we go along, we can combine elements of each, so that our life becomes a journey of continuous discovery. As we practice, we slowly integrate all aspects of our lives and make all our separate members whole again.

Measuring Our Progress

Discouragement will surely come. Some pattern of feelings we thought we had released will return and catch us off guard, and before we know it, we will be treading its familiar rounds. When this happens, remember that you are bigger than your emotions. We are the landscape, not the storm. Use the practices to release the feelings condensed in the pattern. Stick with it until you are in open air again. Remember that the open air is always there.

What can we do, when discouraged, to test whether all our practice makes a difference? When athletes train, their hearts get stronger. Monitoring the heart for the training effect gives an index of how far their training has progressed. When we are out of shape, and then exercise hard, the heart will beat out a rapid rhythm long after we have quit. If we are in good shape, the heart will return to its resting pulse quickly. The more quickly the heart returns to its resting pulse after exercise, the greater the training effect.

Something like this happens as we walk our path, meeting and releasing the beasts in the inscape. There will always be things that can knock us off balance. That does not matter. The question is how quickly we recover. As we practice we recover more quickly. We may find that an old depression that used to last a week now lasts a day. An anger that might have colored an entire weekend now takes an hour and a half. A grudge that would have taken a lifetime takes a few months.

When an old pattern snags us there is nothing to worry about; that is just life as a human being. Instead of being angry, just remember to be grateful that we can release it once again. If it holds us a little less long or less tightly than before, that is already something miraculous.

7

Nature Is
My Teacher

Lost in the Abstract Landscape

Most of us seldom leave the city. We are part of an organizational hierarchy, and we tend to be saturated with entertainment. Our senses attune to these things—to concrete and cars, and the frequently refreshed flicker of computer and video screens.

We seldom walk quietly through woods or desert, watching the life that is lived there. And even if we visit them, we do not know the names of the living things we come upon. We take the rhythms for our bodies and minds from what is around us. We learn our values from those we associate with and what we see. We learn who we are in a series of relationships with the people and other entities we live and work with.

Originally, we tuned ourselves to the change of the seasons and to intimate association with plants, animals, and human beings in the landscape. Without realizing it, we have substituted an abstract ecology for that of the natural world. Instead of watching the cycles of life, and having our experience penetrated by them, we follow the internal requirements of systems that have no natural rhythms.

Within a lifetime, it is probable we can become familiar with only a few landscapes well. An abstract landscape can be assimilated as easily as a natural one, and can come to take its place. Systems of rules are what we learn, rather than systems of living things. They may be the rules of corporate life and behavior, of the stock market, the banking system, the publishing world, the medical and insurance systems, or a thousand others. Instead of planting crops or foraging for food, we go to meetings, write reports, do deals. We come to understand the complexities of the abstract environments the way our ancestors understood the way of the marsh, the woods, the fields. Abstract systems are compelling, even fulfilling. It takes as much care, devotion, intelligence, and skill to become masterful in an abstract as in a natural system.

Any system takes us beyond ourselves. There is a sense of wonder in letting our mind fill the contours of a system. As water fills a vessel and knows its shape by touch, so our mind flows into any system and knows it by moving into the intricacies of its shape. Many brilliant minds find beauty in the complexity of the federal tax code.

Any complex system will give us a sense of discovery and even daring, crossing unknown landscapes alone at great cost to oneself and mapping them in ways no one else has done before. Because abstract systems meet our need to test our skills, we forget what we lose while we live in them: a set of healthy constraints on our work and a way to imbibe wisdom.

The natural landscape is full of constraints. The seasons move at their own pace. Plants and animals grow as they will. Tugging on them does not make them grow faster. When we experience our body and mind as part of the landscape, they also move to a certain rhythm. There is a movement and flow on a deep natural beat.

The abstract landscape we have created has no natural rhythms. The constraints of the seasons do not apply. Instead of matching our work to the rhythms of growing things, we move information. The only constraint on work is the speed with which the information moves. That speed is growing rapidly.

We matched our work to the rhythms of the natural world for millions of years. Absent these rhythms, we do not know how to place limits on ourselves. Many of us are already exhausted from processing information and by the incorporeal demands of the abstract landscape.

We need to find a new way to measure what is reasonable work to do, a way that respects the rhythms of human life. Staring into the distance must be acknowledged as a respectable part of the day. The !Kung bushmen hunt three or four days a week at most and spend much of the rest of their time composing and performing original music, telling stories, and making art. Do they or do we lead the more refined life?

Being lost in the abstract landscape carries a more fundamental problem, too. The natural landscape encodes wisdom; the abstract landscape does not. The abstract landscape is our own product. Residing in the abstract landscape, we live, somewhat autistically, in the projections we have made.

The natural landscape is greater than we are. It has encoded billions of years of wisdom into itself. When we listen to it, we find our rhythms and our place. It is almost impossible to remember this in our culture. Because the vast majority of us live in urban environments and traverse an abstract landscape for our entire working life, remembering natural rhythms seems like a luxury, something that might be valuable but that has nothing to do with the press of daily business. Even environmentalists often tell me they have no time to be in Nature.

As a culture, we are close to retreating into our abstract dream, convinced there is no time to look at the real world. So let us take a walk.

How to Take a Walk

A walk is a chance to imbibe Nature's wisdom. It becomes meditation when we walk slowly, concentrating on our breath, feeling our body move, feeling our feet in contact with the Earth. We can easily let ourselves open and be permeated by this wisdom. It happens in our bodies.

Walk in slow motion. Take a half hour and walk only a hundred yards. As you walk, do your feet fall to touch the Earth, or does the Earth rise to meet them?

Instead of focusing on a single thing, let the attention relax until it broadens to include your whole field of vision. You will begin to see patterns at a scale larger than you would ordinarily see. You might see the wind as waves made visible by its movement through tall grass or through the leaves of trees.

Take the time to let your eyes relax. It may seem strange at first, but in a few moments it will feel natural and will enable you to melt into the landscape.

Become aware of all the life around you: the compact, concentrated life of insects, flowers, and birds. When you come to an insect, a tree, or anything else that calls to you, let your attention go out to it while remaining aware of your awareness.

Let your attention be on the side of the other organism. Go out to it. Let yourself be open to the perceptions of the insect, the flower, the fungus, or whatever it was that called you. Participate in the sense world, the thought world, the experience world of the other.

As you let yourself be open to the world of the other, you begin to get a sense of the strong true life it lives. Let your imagination go out to the life of the other. If a tree, to its patient growth, its feel for the Sun, the taste of water in its soil.

If you are in contact with an ant, let yourself feel the life of that one ant, and the life of its colony, thoroughly. Let yourself know the intelligence of the colony and the sense of belonging to it. Let yourself know what it is like to follow a trail of scent to a source of food and bring back a piece of it for your sisters, a piece as large as yourself.

Get close to the inner life of the beings you meet, even if it feels like a game. As we let ourselves feel the life of other organisms, we get real contact with them and with their perceptions. Their point of view opens to us, and we can receive their teachings. We may begin by feeling how alien these other beings are. We end by having a sense of familiarity, of belonging to the same family.

The more we become intimate with other beings in the landscape, the more we experience the connection between our inner landscape and the outer landscape. We begin to know that our everyday mind is just one specialized form of mind, of which there are many others. When we let the soul come forward, these other forms of mind become more open to us. Knowing them, we are more at home.

When you have had contact with another mind for a while, sense the time to move on. Continue walking in slow motion.

There is always a right time to move on in everything we do in life. We often miss it. Let yourself sense it, thank the other sentient being you were visiting, and move on.

City Life

The ways of mind, heart, and action work wherever we are. Every place is a good place to practice them. They work as well in New York City's Times Square or on a California freeway as they do in a mountain retreat. If this were not true, they would have little value. Their value lies precisely in that they help us to know who we really are in every one of life's circumstances, no matter how difficult.

Some circumstances pose special challenges, city life among them. A happy, relaxed, and open awareness makes it easiest for us to stay fully present in the body and feel the soul come forward. City life challenges our happiness with a swirl of learned desires; our relaxation with stress; our openness with a need to be cautious of safety.

How do we practice with the challenges of city life? By becoming aware of them. City life can be noisy, crowded, stressful in a thousand ways. Do not resist these stresses. Investigate them. Stay in the body, in the present moment. See how you react physically to the noise of a bus going by with its cloud of diesel fumes and to walking in a rush hour crowd. What does it feel like? How do you react in a packed subway car, in a traffic jam, on a checkout line? How do you feel when you meet a panhandler or when someone threatening walks by?

Practice means being fully present wherever our body is, whether we want to be or not. It means being especially attentive to those times when we do not want to be in the body; when we find these nodes of disappearance, we intervene. When we want to be somewhere or someone else, that moment is the richest opportunity to practice. If we are lonely, that is when we practice; if we have been mugged, that is when we practice. Whenever we are uncomfortable, that is when we practice.

Beyond the stress of crowds, noise, and pollution, there is a subtler impact of city life, equally stressful and much harder to see. When we are with people, we are affected by their feelings to a much greater degree than we are usually aware. We are an open flowing system without boundaries. Our systems of perception do not end with the physical body. We are porous; the boundaries between inscape and outscape are fluid. We are susceptible in a high degree to the thoughts and feelings of others.

We all have some awareness of this. At a football game, we share group excitement. A party succeeds when we share a certain kind of feeling. Everyone who has visited New York City knows the specific quality of sharp-edged excitement that is in the air. When we live in a city, we feel the feelings of the group life there. More than likely, we will mistake them for our own. They may even swamp our own.

If we feel depression in a city—or restlessness, loneliness, or sexual neediness—we should ask whose feelings these are. We have to be aware that they may not be "our" feelings at all, even though we register them emotionally. They may be feelings that are widespread in the population, and so we feel them, much as we would the excitement at a football game.

When we have this awareness, we can look into our feelings in a new way. We can ask whether a given feeling arises out of our life, and if so, we can take care of it. If the feeling is arising out of the city and not out of our own life, then we can offer it, and feel it move. When it moves, we will feel a little more compassion for our neighbors and their suffering.

Here are two other practices to work with in the city. They let us feel connected to the natural world in those moments when the city feels overwhelming. The first is to consider the transitory nature of a city.

See the city in your imagination. Now take a ten-thousand-year view. Our cities are fragile, ephemeral constructs. They are not sustainable in their present form, and will be evolving and changing rapidly over the next few hundred years. Taking the ten-thousand-year view, imagine the city evolving, like a coral reef or a forest—a living evolving element in the landscape.

Second, try walking consciously in the city. You can make all your city walking a kind of meditation.

Simply be aware of your feet as they touch the pavement. Consider the pavement the skin of the Earth. Be aware of your feet touching the Earth with every step. That is all there is to it. Awareness with every step. Feel your feet in contact with the Earth.

This is a wonderful practice that can bring calm even at rush hour after a long, hard day. You can do it at any pace, even scrambling for a commuter train. You will also find that it is safe: it makes you more aware, not less aware, of everything going on around you.

Simply be aware of touching the Earth with every step. Try it. It allows us to experience that, just as we are bigger than our feelings, the Earth is bigger than the city. If we are fully aware of each step, everything else in life will start to take care of itself.

Talking with What Lives

We can talk with all that lives. Most of us have forgotten how to do this, but we can all relearn it. The language of our ancestors did not end at the edge of human conversation. The other living beings around them were all part of a conversational community. The wisdom tales in indigenous cultures are the stories told by raven, coyote, and the other creatures. We may think our ancestors were making myth when they talked in this way, but that is because we have forgotten how to hear. When we remember, we begin to live the inner truth of myth and everything is full of life again.

There is a German myth that could come from any other indigenous tribe. In the story, crane shows us how to write. Crane teaches us the alphabet by leaving the marks of its long toes incised on soft clay.

We can reawaken our ability to hear the language of other beings by participation, by softening the barrier between subject and object, by merging with what we seek to know. This is what the mystics do.

There is a story of an Indian holy man that shows how fully one can participate. One day he was walking past a field and saw a farmer beating a bullock with a whip. The holy man's heart went out to the bullock so strongly that *his* back was scored with the welts raised by the farmer's blows.

We can open to the experience of the trout in its stream. We can know what the water feels like on its glistening skin, what it is like to swim in the delicious cold current and catch a mayfly. We can open to the salmon, and to the bear that eats it. We can open to the grove of aspen and experience its vastness, know what it feels like to be one great entity covering a quarter of a mile underground and manifesting as myriad individual trees.

We are all native speakers of the language of life. Go outside; listen to the birds and hear their language. Listen to the insects and hear what they have to say. Listen to the mammals and grasses, to the trees and spiders. If it comes to you, let yourself be a praying mantis. It is a wonderful experience. When you are a praying mantis, milky jade in the welcoming sun, you are the only insect that can turn its head and look over its shoulder. So turn and look.

To talk with what lives, we have to listen patiently and quietly and for a long time. We have to listen in a place where we can hear, where the sounds of the living world are louder than the sounds of the machine world. If we have the patience and the silence we can begin to hear. If many of us listen, many of us will hear. We will learn the language of the living Earth, and it will become our language again.

Alone With

There is a dialogue of wave and rain that happens at the ocean's shore. We can hear it only after entering the profound silence of the alone with.

Alone with what is, alone with what breathes, alone with what erodes through millennia. Alone with the warbler, who has knocked into the plate glass window after flying a thousand miles in migration. Alone with the warbler's mild concussion. Standing near it, appreciating the intense sulfur of its breast, the feathers of its back composed of intricate green smoke, heart going out to it.

Alone with the warbler as the jay flashes in from nowhere silently, and in the time and space of an eyeblink is away with the warbler between its beak. Alone with the loss, the speed, the precision of Nature's dispositions.

Alone again with the sea and the rain. The continuous, sustaining pulse of the ocean, playing its endless music of crash and go. A lush and ceaseless pounding, then a pointillist rush of stone on stone by waves as they recede, their sound running up the scale and down in volume into hush. Alone with the softer sustenance of rain, sweetwater as it falls, sounding its palette of plashes, playing its touch to fern on a different note from its touch to pine and stone.

Alone with the jay as it streaks screaming back through,

cackling the intention of its next meal, in strident contrast to the water sounds. Sounds that can be heard only in the profound silence of the alone with.

An alone with that we can share with another once we have entered into it. An alone with that we can return to whenever it is shattered. An alone with that is finally so familiar we live in it always, and bring it always with us, even into Times Square.

Because we are alone with, we see and hear. Because we are alone with, we can open our heart. Once we have been alone with, we are never lonely again.

Deep Silence

In silence the mind clarifies. In silence the heart opens. We seldom experience silence. Yet after love and food, silence is what sustains us most.

The landscape for most of us is an urban area where noise abounds. Noise rolls at us in great waves from the engines of cars, trucks, buses, jets, lawn mowers, leaf blowers, and on and on. We watch TVs and patch CDs into our ears. We have gotten used to a loud aural landscape. New restaurants are designed with a high noise level to make people feel comfortable.

The noise in our outer landscape has increased markedly in the last few decades. Until recently, what we heard most was the unamped human voice. Louder environments were found mostly on battlefields, in factories, and near brass bands. There was much relative quiet—and a lot less human stress. Physiologically, noise causes stress, whether we know it or not.

When I lived in Los Angeles, I often felt cramped by the sprawl and lonely for animals, plants, and insects in a more natural world. One day I climbed a peak north of the city to feel my life. Sitting on the peak, I heard the soft, tearing sound of a raven's wing part the air as it soared past. It had been a long time since I had heard the sound of a bird's wing cutting through the liquid medium of air.

Not long ago I heard a skylark sing, and it was glorious. A liquescent falling sound that tumbled down as the lark lifted into the sky and soared. Its song fell as a curtain of notes, delimiting its territory with an evanescent, musical gesture. The song of the lark transformed the cold bare fields in northern Germany where I heard it. I stopped to listen, and then heard the silence that followed the skylark's song.

We are seldom silent with each other. Yet what follows silence is wonderful. When I enter silence with someone, they often share what they have hidden, even from themselves. When we enter silence, it comes gently, like soft rain on parched ground. Hidden seeds begin to sprout that need silence to germinate and would never grow in noise.

Silence allows an intimacy words do not. It is a pleasure to construct no social mask for a while when we sit with someone in silence. We get a feel for the masks we wear this way and for who we are without them.

Silence will bring us beyond pretense if we allow it to. As we let it grow in our lives, we can begin to touch the heart of anyone who is sincere in a way we thought possible only with a few. As silence deepens, we engage less and less with those who are insincere.

In our culture, inner silence is a radical act. Once we experience it, we are changed. There is being in silence, and there is melting into silence. There is hearing silence, and the hearing that silence brings us. There is tasting silence, and what we taste in silence is often the first taste. There is seeing in silence, and there is revelation in it always. In these ways we see into the outer more deeply, see the boundary we build between inscape and outscape, and also see that it is porous. Inner silence begins to let us see clearly.

The clarity will often surprise us. The doorways of perception can be simply cleansed. And though it feels as though time is being expended, inner silence reveals that our clarity was always there waiting patiently for us to use it. In inner

silence we know that the world is created again in every
moment out of nothing, continuously. In inner silence the
mind pauses in an astonishment so delicate it has no words. In
its rapture, the mind learns to observe what emerges from the
unknowable. Observing, it says, "This is what I always
sought!"

When the mind knows inner silence, it can stop its struggles and turn its attention to appreciation, which is the source
of all understanding. It is then the heart can open.

One Square Foot

When we give our attention we give love. When we do this with no thought for ourselves, we reside in open mind and heart. We merge with and participate in whatever we attend to. We encounter a more yielding reality than we ordinarily know, and can receive its teachings.

It can all happen in one square foot of Earth. Try it. Take yourself outdoors and find a place where things grow. A city park or a wilderness will do equally well. Choose a season when things are alive and growing.

> *Find a square foot of Earth. Sit or lie down beside it in a comfortable posture you can maintain for an hour. Mark your square foot out with rocks or twigs at the corners. Now pay unwavering attention to what lives in that one square foot.*
>
> *See what is there. Much of it will be at a smaller scale than you usually notice. Do not touch anything, just attune your senses. Watch, listen, smell. Follow your curiosity. Watch everything. There is a universe at every level of scale.*

Darwin once did an experiment with three tablespoons of pond soil. He grew all the plants he could out of those three tablespoons, and counted 537 of them. On a smaller scale yet, were you to take a pinch of soil from your square foot, you would hold about 10 billion bacteria between thumb and forefinger.

Study your one square foot of Earth. What is alive there? What plants, what insects? Are there any worms or snails? Spiders?

It will take about twenty minutes of looking before you really start to see. By then you begin to move with the internal rhythms of the beings within your one square foot. Something you thought dead or inorganic will startle you with a movement so subtle you would never have noticed it before.

Let yourself experience the life world of the beings in your one square foot. Your awareness is love, and loving anything can bring you to the whole. If a question arises in your heart, let it rise. Ask it.

One of my students found her one square foot on a misty day. Wearing rain gear, she lay down on her belly in a grassy field. She made her one square foot in a vertical plane, like a picture frame around a stand of tall grass. At first she studied the grass, moisture like lenses where it collected into drops, concentrating and refracting the whole of what surrounded her. She then gave her awareness to wildflowers, blue, tiny, vivid, growing with the grass.

Only then, after maybe twenty minutes, did she notice the caterpillar. It had been there all along, but she had not seen it. As she studied the caterpillar, a question came out of her heart.

With absolute sincerity, she asked the caterpillar, "Please teach me the nature of metamorphosis."

"Why should I teach you the nature of metamorphosis?" the caterpillar replied.

"Because you know all about it," she said.

"What makes you think so?" the caterpillar asked.

"Because you are certain to go through a complete meta-morphosis yourself," she said, wondering why she had to explain this to a caterpillar. "You will spin a cocoon, your body will dissolve and remake itself, and you will one day emerge as a butterfly."

"There is no certainty in that," said the caterpillar. "Most of us never make it that far. We are either eaten by predators or fail to find the right food plants. Either way, most of us die as caterpillars. You, on the other hand, as a human being, have a whole lifetime full of metamorphosis. You grow and change constantly. To find out about metamorphosis, you should study yourself!"

Her experience is the kind of thing that happens when we study what lives in one square foot. We experience for our-selves the way in which stillness opens perception and leads to magic. We appreciate that when the heart asks its questions from deep silence they are received and subtly answered. And we learn that inscape and outscape are part of the same con-tinuum, as my student learned on her belly in the grass.

Teachings from a Moth

On our land in Santa Fe, Martin was stopped by the sight of a moth one day. It was hanging low in a juniper, on a branch near the ground. The summer afternoon was late and goldeny. He called me back and I knelt down.

The moth was a little tatty. The edges of its front wings, its overwings, were frayed as if it had flown far, found a mate, and was resting, tired, for the final evening's flight of its brief life. Its wings were folded on the left side, so that the brown overwing concealed the underwing. But on the right-hand side, the overwing was raised and exposed its bright surprise.

The underwing disclosed an enormous eye. To achieve the full effect, I gently moved the left overwing, exposing the paired eye on the other side.

Suddenly, an owl's full face jumped out in three dimensions. The eyes were huge, cerulean shading to midnight. In each circle was a streak of white, as of light entering into the viscid depth of the owl's pupil. The white streak was blurred slightly where a beam would be blurred by the aqueous humor in the depths of the eye's globe. Under the eyes were the owl's golden cheek feathers, and then a brown and reddish line delimiting its cheeks, giving the effect of depth and shadow. The owl's beak was cunningly rendered: the moth's fat body, tapering down between the wings, was set off on its flanks with shadow colors, and gave the effect of a thick sharp beak standing out between the eyes.

It was an Io moth, named after one of the many maidens who had an unhappy affair with Zeus.

> *Imagine now that you are a mouse who has spotted a fat brown tasty moth sitting, wings folded, in a juniper waiting for the night. This moth will be an extravagant meal for you, a real delight, a rare night out.*
>
> *You approach, stomach juices churning with expectation. Out of nowhere appears your worst nightmare. Only inches away! Owls are so swift, so silent, so deadly!*

Whence this perfect mimicry? How can the moth reach so far for the owl's pattern: not only across species, but across phyla, from insect to bird? How can it reach across this genetic ocean to pluck from Nature's memory the perfect image of its predator's predator?

How can the moth and its insect genes find their way into the relationship between the mouse and the owl at all? It cannot, if the moth is a species that exists in isolation, as we tend to think of species. It is not enough to say that the owl's face appeared in its perfection on the moth's wings by the accumulation of random changes, approximating a useful pattern.

Consider this thoroughly: the owl's face on the insect's wings displays the relationship between the mammal and bird. Members of these phyla are radically different, as our science treats them. And yet they live in a ring of relationship. The owl's face on the moth is an emblem of this relationship, and of understanding it. When the moth flashes its hind wings, it is making a joke in deadly earnest. The pattern displayed has meaning for the mouse because of the syntax of the mouse-moth-owl relationship.

The mouse, the moth, and the owl are not separate

species: they are just mouse-moth-owl. Both the moth and the owl reach into the same locus in the implicate order for the pattern they share, which lies deep below their relationship.

The Io moth reaches for its owl pattern across all boundaries: nothing in Nature could resist answering it. Its reach is the same as ours when we enter into the Eureka Practice and ask for a solution.

Mind, matter, and energy are not separate. Asking opens a well within us into which all the information in the Universe needed for the answer flows across all space and time.

What Gilgamesh Was
Afraid Of

The *Epic of Gilgamesh*, a poem five thousand years old, was preserved on clay tablets discovered only in the last century. The first surviving epic, antedating Homer by a millennium and a half, it tells the story of a great king of the city of Uruk, built with thick walls on the Euphrates between Babylon to the north and Ur to the south. The biblical name for the city is Erech.

Gilgamesh comes to vivid life in the poem, in which he is depicted as strong and courageous beyond measure. Not only can no man match him in arms; he turns down a goddess as his consort, and journeys to the abode of the gods for the elixir of eternal life before learning that death comes even to the mighty.

Gilgamesh is a hero's hero. His adventure still speaks powerfully to us today as we try to understand our relationship with the Earth. What was this initial adventure of the first tragic hero of whom anything is known? It was a forest journey. He went with his boon companion into the heart of the sacred cedar forest, there to kill the forest guardian and cut down the forest.

The forest guardian is a giant called Humbaba, or Hugeness. He is armed with:

sevenfold terrors, terrible to all flesh. . . . When he
roars it is like the torrent of the storm, his breath is
like fire, and his jaws are death itself. . . . What man
would willingly walk into that country and explore its
depths? . . . The watchman of the forest never sleeps.

Hearing of the forest and its guardian, Gilgamesh has his
armourers cast a great ax called Might of Heroes, and determines to enter into the forest:

I, Gilgamesh, go to see that creature of whom such
things are spoken, the rumor of whose name fills the
world. I will conquer him in his cedar wood, and show
the strength of the sons of Uruk, all the world shall
know of it. I am committed to this enterprise: to climb
the mountain, to cut down the cedar, and leave behind
me an enduring name.

Gilgamesh and his companion, Enkidu, journey to the forest. Reaching it,

they stood still, they were struck dumb; they stood
still and gazed at the forest. They saw the height
of the cedar. . . . The hugeness of the cedar rose in
front of the mountain, its shade was beautiful, full of
comfort. . . .

Gilgamesh, however, has come to cut down the forest, not
to enjoy it. He enters and cuts a tree. Humbaba, the forest
guardian, who can hear a heifer lowing at sixty leagues,

heard the noise far off [and] was enraged; he cried out,
"Who is this that has violated my woods and cut down
my cedar?"

When Gilgamesh sees Humbaba, he is afraid, "and his tears were flowing." He calls out to his god, who binds Humbaba with the eight winds, leaving him at Gilgamesh's mercy. When Humbaba sees what has happened to him, he surrenders, and says:

> . . . all the trees of the forest that I tended on the mountain shall be yours. I will cut them down and build you a palace.

Gilgamesh is moved, and decides to spare the forest guardian. His companion, Enkidu, argues against compassion. "Kill him," Enkidu argues, "or he will lie ever in wait for you, to attack when you least expect it."

Gilgamesh answers that there is something great in Humbaba they should not extinguish but protect now that he is in their power. Gilgamesh says:

> If we touch him the blaze and the glory of light will be put out in confusion, the glory and glamour will vanish, its rays will be quenched.

"Not so," says Enkidu. "Kill him and cut down the forest, and the glory and glamour will be yours."

Gilgamesh listens to Enkidu. He kills Humbaba the forest guardian, and:

> For as far as two leagues the cedars shivered. . . . Now the mountains were moved and all the hills, for the guardian of the forest was killed.

Then Gilgamesh and Enkidu began to fell the forest: "They attacked the cedars, the seven splendors of Humbaba were extinguished." And so the glory and the glamour were gone.

This, then, is the first and greatest act of the first epic hero: to enter the sacred forest, kill the guardian, and fell the trees. The entire history of the West in its relation with the Earth is prefigured in this story. Gilgamesh is the Adam of the ecological age.

Moreover, his is a more complex morality tale than the story of Adam eating the apple. Here we have the hero Gilgamesh, with the power of life and death over the great forest guardian, representing everything fearful in the psyche. While he is confident of being in control, Gilgamesh decides to release Humbaba and let him live "like a snared bird returned to the nest." Had the story ended here, we would have a story of triumph over the fear of our own inner shadows and of harmony with the Earth.

Enkidu enters the arena of Gilgamesh's forbearance, however, to speak for fear and greed. These turn Gilgamesh from compassion to murder. "Do not trust him," says Enkidu, an early avatar of Iago. "You can never trust the forest guardian. He works on behalf of the forest, and all that lies concealed within it. If you spare him, he will kill you when you are not looking."

Gilgamesh is not yet capable of murder, and argues with Enkidu. "If I kill him I will kill something precious, glorious, glamorous," says Gilgamesh, not wanting to do it. When Enkidu argues that Gilgamesh can have these powers for himself by killing Humbaba, greed augments fear, and Gilgamesh loses his hold on compassion.

The temptation Gilgamesh succumbs to is not gaining the knowledge of good and evil but gaining Humbaba's marvelous intimacy with and control of the natural world, should he kill him. He then succumbs, kills Humbaba, cuts the forest, and the magic begins to drain from the world.

Gilgamesh prefigures us all, is emblematic of us all, and acts for us all. He feels some sympathy for the natural world when it is at his mercy. He then allows his fear of it to rise, and believes he will gain its power for himself if he destroys it. He breaks faith with the world of Nature, whose glory and glamour he acutely feels, cuts down the forest, and calls it the deed of a hero.

Recall my prayer in the sweat lodge: "Let us not cut down the forests in our hearts, out of fear of the beasts who dwell in them." This fear is the central fact for Gilgamesh. It is the fulcrum that Enkidu uses to turn him from compassion. Because he fears the forest in the inscape, he cuts down the forest in the outscape.

Whence this fear? We are mammals descended from savanna dwellers. We left the forests for the open grasslands millions of years ago, but our genes remember. In psychological studies, human beings of all ethnic backgrounds prefer scenes of open savanna to woods. Our genes remember the dangers of the forest and want open country, so we can see our predators coming.

The English country manor is a temperate savanna hacked from oak forests. Le Nôtre's gardens at Versailles, Italian Renaissance gardens, and American suburban lawns all share this savanna quality. The Japanese, in an island-evolved variation, reduce gardens to open fields of stone, or else prune trees into low shrubs and the see-through shapes of savanna trees. The great forests of Greece and Rome were all felled by classical times. And the Roman soldiers marching into Germany were terrified of Teutonic pine forests, of which only a relict population now remains.

We cut down the trees wherever we go, making savanna to dwell in, so we can see the lions our genes remember should they one day come to hunt us. We fear forests, their darkness, the beasts that can lurk in them and leap at us with no warning. It is not only economic greed coupled with ignorance that motivates human beings to cut down forests beyond all need of reason, although these have much to do with it. It is also this ancient fear. Fear below the threshold of our awareness is as strong a driver as greed and ignorance can ever be.

In cutting the rain forest, we are only continuing what Gilgamesh began. To the multinational executives in Tokyo, working hard to open roads over the Andes so they can clear-cut the pristine forest of the Amazonian province of Rhondonia, it must seem that they, too, are doing a heroic deed. A heroic deed that will end, as does the Gilgamesh poem, in tragedy.

We can preserve forests only by maturing beyond our genetic memory of and preference for savannas, by getting over our fear of forest darkness. This does not mean giving up savanna aesthetics, only releasing the shadow of our instinctual fixation on them, with the cascade of depredation it unleashes unawares.

How can we do this? By the same, certain methods that allow us to grow beyond all instinctually driven behavior that no longer serves us. That is, by the slow patient process of bringing the material into our awareness, looking into its roots, and releasing it, thereby releasing ourselves. It is the method of awakening, in all matters great and small.

And so we walk into the forests of our hearts, meeting the beasts that dwell in them and releasing them. What we do in the world reflects and grows out of what we do in our heart. To heal our action in the outscape, we need to heal our action in the inscape. This is why we practice.

The Scorpion in the Water Glass

The scorpion in the water glass on my desk was hiding behind the shutters the other day. Relishing a diet of flies, he is keeping me company for a few days, and then will have to catch his own food again.

He is small, just three-quarters of an inch long when folded in upon himself; he doubles in length when he holds his claws forward and his tail straight out behind. His claws, back, and tail are a rich, dark, high-cocoa-content-chocolate brown. His legs and stinger are a light tan and almost translucent. He wears Chanel colors from the forties. Though his sight is dim he perceives vibrations, as of an insect on the ground, with preternatural acuity, aided by comblike organs called pectens slung under the belly. He sits there complete within himself, full of scorpion mind, more beautiful than any work of humans. Yet we fear him.

Let us look more deeply into our fears of the natural world. We often cover such fears with culture. A Japanese monk once explained to me why there is no beauty in untamed Nature. Only when the natural world is trained into the contours of a garden does it become beautiful. He regarded my contrary feelings as incomprehensible, or at least untutored. Perhaps the monk's notion, culturally derived, covers a fear of wildness. A fear of being out of control and in danger as soon as we step from the civilized into the wild.

> *Let yourself become aware of your fear of the natural world. Imagine going into the mountains, or wherever your imagination takes you. Enter that terrain. See what you are afraid of. What is it?*
>
> *Let yourself know you are safe and let the fear arise fully, right into your gorge. What is the fear? Let yourself find its shape and form. Name it.*
>
> *When you have named it, stop, turn around, and stop running from it. It is only fear. Befriend it. Get to know it. It already knows you well. Take it for a walk.*

A few years ago, I asked what I was afraid of in this way. When I had named it, it was this: to walk into the woods on a moonless night and challenge all my demons to attack me. Having named the fear, it was time to meet it.

I selected a low mountain nearby, covered in mature beech woods, with a path through the trees winding to the top. I waited for the next new Moon so the night would be dark. Entering the woods, I followed the path up. The beeches towering above soaked up the starlight, and the night was truly dark, visibility approaching nil.

I began to feel fear, and offered the fear as I climbed the mountain. Walking and breathing, feet touching the Earth. Near the top I turned and addressed my demons in a loud voice: "I am alone in the woods in the dark without even a light. This is your best chance. I am unprotected. I call you forth now: if you are ever going to attack or challenge me, do it now or forever know you are defeated!"

As the invocation died into silence, my fear grew. The hair on the nape of my neck stood on end, electric. Then, all at once, I felt a tsunami of fear rush at me from the dark. I offered it, called on the Divine, and waited. The wave swept over me and was gone. It was only fear. It was named, it was met, it was done with.

We can each run this kind of experiment with our own fear of the natural world. Look into the fear, name it, meet it. It may be as simple as picking up a spider in a glass and releasing it instead of killing it next time you find one in the kitchen. To pick up and release a spider in this way may take courage, and the courage will be rewarded, always, by a feeling of greater strength. As we get over our fears of the natural world, we can relax into our bodies more, feel our feelings more, be more truly ourselves.

One morning in Santa Fe, Martin reached for a glass of water by the bed. As he raised it, he was startled into wakefulness by a black widow in the water. The black widow was dead; perhaps she had fallen in overnight. What would you feel if you found a black widow in the water glass? It is possible to feel fascination. What would you do to get through your fears and find the fascination? If we cannot release these fears, we cannot be fully present in our bodies on the Earth. Until this happens, how can we enjoy being fully human or embody a positive vision of the future?

The Samurai and
the Nightingale

The samurai is soft as the water that washes away stone over the course of an eon; the nightingale is tough as nails. This is the other side of their more obvious, opposite aspects. Fully present in their bodies, they are each a single motion flowing in stillness. Entirely accepting of what they are, there is no separation within them. They are as intimate with themselves as cloudshadow with the grasses it meets passing over a field. Accepting everything about themselves, knowing this body is enough, samurai and nightingale express the whole without boundaries. A rattlesnake is like this. The Sun is like this. The Universe as a whole, one great body fully awakened, is like this.

In silence we move past the conflict of opposites. In stillness all levels of our being function unhindered. In our full presence in the body, the Universe enjoys itself through us.

Be silent.

Be still.

Be fully present in the body.

Be as soft as the samurai and as tough as the nightingale. And also the opposite, simultaneously and without conflict.

On Being Shattered, or the Lobster's Tale

Lobsters are irritable, like I am; perhaps that is one reason I like them. My enthusiasm for arthropods is boundless, though, so I would probably like lobsters even if they had more personal charm. Their irritability may stem, at least in part, from the fact that as they go through life, lobsters must step out of their shell to grow. Their thick integument of chitinous skin, the same stuff that makes up our fingernails and a beetle's back, is also their skeleton. For the lobster, and for spiders and insects, the skeleton is on the outside, which is a bit inconvenient for growth.

Perhaps our experience is not so different. As we go through life, we have the experience of being shattered again and again. Each time, an aspect of our personality that had become calcified into shell is broken open. It reconfigures again, and eventually begins to calcify. If we have committed ourselves to a path, our existing constructs will be shattered each time they harden into shell.

Each time we reach a place of seeming stability, we will be shattered. When we come to a place of knowing who we are and what we want, that too will be shattered. For every construct we live by, for each personality we adopt seriatim, there is a shattering, so that we can grow.

The only constant we experience is growth and change.

The snake can shed its skin. The lobster and spider must step out of theirs. The very skin that protected them and held them in equipoise with gravity. And the lobster's skin is thick, thicker than the spider's, because the weight of the sea adds pressure to gravity. Both lobster and spider must allow the external skeleton to break open, and then step out. The body thus exposed is soft and vulnerable. Among lobsters, which tend toward cannibalism as well as irritability, to step out of your shell means you may be eaten by another lobster. But you do it anyway, compelled by the need to grow.

Our personality is the armature that our awareness uses to move through the world. We employ a personality at each point in our evolution and growth. We have serial personalities. We exude them like a lobster its shell. Our mistake is to think that we are them. This mistake leads us to believe we must defend the personality and maintain it, at a great expense of energy.

Growth requires that we surrender this idea again and again. We come to a place where our personality feels too tight. A deep pattern presents itself and our personality is at a loss. There may be a premonition of the shedding to come, and we may withdraw, like a lobster finding a safe hole. When we are ready to become bigger than the armature that supports us, it must be shattered, and we must shed it. It is only our armature that is shattered. Our soul is undisturbed, ready to produce a larger skin. The shattering of our old skin requires only that we admit with absolute sincerity that we need to get bigger.

There is always the terror of stepping out of our old protective skin. But a new one will reliably extrude itself. And even though the new skin allows a bigger view, we will again make the mistake of taking it for who we are. So the growth and shattering goes on. Our heart is broken open, again and again, until it is big enough to hold the world.

The Horse of Bone

Between the ages of six and sixteen, Mary Queen of Scots lived in a chateau west of Paris at Saint-Germain-en-Laye. The chateau is now the National Museum of Antiquities, at the limit of the Metro. There I met the horse of bone.

It was in an exhibition of prehistoric sculpture found in caves in the Pyrenees and dating from around 12,000 B.C. The horse's head, broken off near the top of the neck, is in an otherwise excellent state of preservation and has a patina that only millennia can bring. The head is small: five centimeters from mouth to neck, three from the tip of the ear to the bottom of the jaw. The sculpture when entire would have fit beautifully in the hand. An urgency stirs in this head: the ears are held back, and the mouth is open, as if the horse were rearing back and neighing.

Meeting this horse draws forward other horses we know. Tang horses in terra-cotta; the horses in Picasso's *Guernica*. When the Tang and *Guernica* horses join the horse of bone, we realize they are all members of the same herd. All equally expressive, real, full of the essence of horseness. The ancient horse is achieved with a mastery of expression and technique fully equal to those of the Chinese and modern masters. This small lump of bone gives us the visceral experience that our ancestors, the ones who went into the sacred caves, were fully as human as we.

Why did they go into the caves? Why did they paint and sculpt images of horses and bison, aurochs and rhinos, great cats and bears? The painted grottoes were not just living space. Often they are much too deep for that. At Niaux in the Pyrenees, some of the great frescoes are more than a mile in. Nor were they just making magic, trying to ensure a good hunt. Most of the paintings, after all, are of animals they never ate.

Let us make contact with cave art. When we do this, we begin to really see this art. We sense that these ancestors were fellow Earth mystics and that they went deep into the womb of the Earth for a sacred purpose: to meet the Other, to know the Other, to learn from the Other.

Our ancestors went into the caves to meet the beasts in the forests of their hearts. They went to be silent, to be still, to be fully present in the Body of the Earth. For them, going into the caves was entering the inscape. Dark, rich, fearful until mastered. The caves were an experience of the inscape made manifest.

Imagine yourself there, fourteen thousand years ago, ready to enter a sacred cave. One that human beings have already been visiting in this way for ten thousand years. You are dressed in skins sewn together with an ivory needle and rawhide thread. You are only thirty, but already an elder. You have had dreams recently of a great cat stalking the tribe. The cat is larger than a Bengal tiger and is bent on killing human beings in the dark. It is time to go and meet this cat, and it is for this you enter the cave.

With two young assistants, you pray to the Earth. You carry paints, charcoal and ochre and hematite, and your assistants carry flickering pine torches. You climb down and down. More than a mile in, you find the gallery that called you, and you stand before a wall covered with paintings of horses and bear. You stand in prayer, asking the Earth to move through you. When you feel her energy clearly, you invoke the cat. You call to it in absolute sincerity, out of deep silence.

The cat comes. You walk through the doorway of fear, because your people need you to. You meet the cat and ask it what it needs. You feel the cat's soul, its energy, its knowledge. The compelling and coherent energy of its life, as clear and close as your own.

While you are full of the cat, you pick up your paints and let the cat move through you, drawing itself on the wall through your arm, your hand, your eye. The cat draws not one but six cats, a pride, a hunting group, its tribe just like yours. When you put down your paints, you are the cat and it is you. For always from then on.

And now let yourself visit a cathedral in your mind. Walk around it, dark and spacious and cool. Notice how the cathedral is like a sacred cave our ancestors erected on the plain. The place to go for silence and stillness, and to meet the Other. A cave with rose windows now, to let in the light, to encourage us as we meet the beasts in the forests of our hearts. A cave to enter in which we can explore the inscape with the help of guides.

Caves and cathedrals were the spaces our ancestors used to meet the beasts. Caves were an exteriorization of the inscape; cathedrals evolved from caves, bringing the cave into the town and opening it to more light. Both caves and cathedrals are in our past. We can taste the human life lived there, but they are no longer ours. They are wombs we cannot reenter.

What is the next turn in this evolution from cave to cathedral? Perhaps we no longer need to project the inscape onto cave or cathedral, because we can range in it at will. We can now stand naked and exposed in the open air of Earth. Knowing the inscape, we can directly meet the beasts in the forests of our hearts. We can invoke them, meet and release them, thereby freeing ourselves.

Gaia is the only cathedral we need. All of Gaia is sacred space. It is all around us, wherever we are, always. We need only open, meet, release, and be. In this way, we bring freedom into the midst of the world for the sake of all beings.

Doing this, let us remember our ancestors. They went hungry in the desert; they were cold on mountains; they went fearful into the womb of Earth. They were tough and magnificent, and we are their successors. Let us ask for their help with a clear intention, and let them succeed through us, so that we may bring wisdom into the world for the sake of all beings.

8

Toward
Homo Gaians

Entering into Gaia

We will now see how our awakening relates to the Earth and to our emergence as a new global species: *Homo gaians*. Let us orient ourselves by sharing a story of Gaia, the living Earth. Recall that vital myth combines the human quest to know who we are with the best science of the times in images that situate us in a landscape of meaning.

Gaia theory says that a superorganism emerges out of all the life on Earth, much as our body emerges out of all our living cells. The superorganism Gaia maintains global conditions equable for life by regulating the gases in the atmosphere, the temperature, the salinity of the oceans, and so on, much as our body keeps the right balance of blood sugar, the right temperature, and other internal conditions fit for life. Gaia, however, consists of more than just the living biota. It emerges out of the totality of living things and all the inorganic material that life uses, depends on, transforms, and co-evolves with. So atmospheric gases, water, granite, oceanic salts, and sulfur are all part of Gaia, just as the calcium in our bones is part of our body.

James Lovelock, the founder of Gaia theory, calls it a theory of geophysiology; conservative scientists who twitch with discomfort at the word *Gaia* have nevertheless started calling themselves geophysiologists. Because Gaia theory is the best

geophysiology of our time, it appeals to our mind; because it
names an entity that acts with general benignity toward life,
it appeals to our heart. When we seek to see how our human
life fits into this newly understood global pattern of meaning,
we experience vital myth.

> *Sit by the fire in a European cave on the southern bor-*
> *der of the last ice age, while the person sitting next to*
> *you sculpts a horse of bone. Or by a campfire on the*
> *African savanna, in the Australian outback, or wher-*
> *ever else your mind takes you.*
>
> *Feel the warmth of the Ur-campfire around which,*
> *by telling stories, we first became conscious of being*
> *human.*
>
> *Now let yourself see the Earth from space, a circle*
> *of vivid blue suspended in the enfolding empty velvet*
> *blackness, life blooming in the void, improbable, lush,*
> *compelling, necessary. Let yourself appreciate this blue,*
> *and also the white of the clouds as they move with*
> *steady grace over the oceans and the land. Feel how*
> *precious, what a jewel beyond price, is the living Earth*
> *as it moves through the emptiness of space.*
>
> *This is the body of Gaia.*

Now come down closer and enter into Gaia's body:

> *Let yourself stand in a desert, a towering thunderhead*
> *before you in the enormous sky. See lightning rend the*
> *sky from top to bottom, like a crack in our Universe*
> *open to a blinding beyond. Hear great claps of thunder.*
> *Feel their percussion move the ground like earthquake.*
> *See the rain as it begins to fall in wide loud pounding*
> *drops. Smell the perfumes it draws up from the desert,*
> *ripe to receive it. Hear the seeds of desert flowers as*
> *they burst and begin to sprout.*

When you have seen and heard and smelled these things, imagine yourself kneeling in the rain forest:

Feel the moisture of the Earth against your kneecaps. Smell the richness of the air, carrying the commingled scents of a thousand flowers, further enriched with rot, the encouraging odor of decomposing life. Hear the wild calls of birds and baboons. Turn your head and look up at the trees towering over you; then look lower to see a blue Morpho butterfly, giant and azure, iridesce in a beam of sunlight breaking through the canopy. Now follow the beam down to the ground before you, and as you kneel watch a procession of leafcutter ants carry neatly cut bits of leaf back to the fungus gardens in their nest.

When you have seen and heard and smelled these things, imagine yourself standing on a California coastal hill.

Let yourself see the ocean before you and a great city to the south. Catch the fresh, salty, iodine-laced ocean air; watch a pod of whales swim by; hear the ocean; and enjoy the regularity of the waves. Now, turning left toward the city, see the movement of distant cars, like blood cells through capillaries. And now, smell the aroma of garlic cooking in olive oil, ever a call to appetite, as it wafts over you from a café just behind.

All these things, and we ourselves, are embodied thoughts of Gaia.

Now, having seen the body of Gaia and experienced some of the embodied thoughts of Gaia, let us see into the mind of Gaia. The mind of Gaia is huge, built on a different scale than ours. Its single goal is to nurture life, and yet it is impersonal.

Its earliest memories are three and a half billion years old. It has never been bored and never needed entertainment.

The mind of Gaia is endlessly fascinated by increasing the diversity of life and the complexity of its organization. It thinks at thousands of interpenetrating levels simultaneously and worldwide. It enjoys itself as billions of nested differential equations solving themselves in matter in real time in every moment. It improvises itself as a trillion-part fugue that self-replicates, with variations. It knows itself as the death into birth of organic beings without number through time.

The terms of Gaia's mind are every living thing, and its goal is an abundance of life moving through time into ever greater levels of diversity and ever more subtle levels of complex and stable organization.

Gaia's mind sees things as patterns of light. It sees every species as a pathway of energy and light. There are no static elements, only pathways of energy and light.

Watch now, as the Sun pours light into the atmosphere. Some is reflected by clouds, some absorbed by the algae in the ocean and by the plants on land.

Imagine the light of the Sun as it enters the atmosphere and is absorbed by plants. See the plants as small points of light, absorbing it, and then passing it on, light flowing through to whatever eats the plants. See a beetle eat a leaf, see the light flow from the leaf into the beetle. See a warbler eat the beetle, and watch the light flow into the warbler. See a goshawk eat the warbler, and watch the light flow into the goshawk.

See the goshawk die, fall to the ground on a border between forest and cornfield, and begin to decompose. See the light move into the maggots and bacteria that feed on the goshawk. See the light move into the spider that eats the fly newly hatched from the goshawk's chest, now open to the sky, and into the mouse that eats the spider. Into the larger bacteria that eat the smaller in the body of the goshawk. Into the corn plant that absorbs the nutrients from the goshawk's body that the bacteria decompose into soil. Into the child that eats corn on the cob, butter running down his round, packed cheeks.

The Tapestry of Life and Light

Seeing the energy of the Sun pour into the Earth, let yourself see its movement through organic beings as a loom of light energy, moving up through the warp and woof of life. Each individual creature is a flow of light through time, a thread in the ever changing tapestry of light. Each species is a pattern of light that emerges in the tapestry as it is woven over eons. The pattern of every species is a focus in the flow of light, and the design in the tapestry grows subtler and more complex as new species evolve over three and a half billion years. This tapestry of life and light is the mind of Gaia; its elaboration into complex and stable patterns is the joy of Gaia; weaving the tapestry itself is the goal of Gaia.

Gaia regulates the mix of gases in the atmosphere, the temperature of the planet, the salinity of the ocean, the rainfall and cloud cover, the transformation of volcanic basalt and water into life-supporting granite, plate tectonics. It does all this so that the tapestry of life can be woven, just as our body works to maintain itself so that we can live and reproduce. For Gaia, there is birth and death and also no birth and death. Every organism and every species are Gaia; when any individual or species dies, part of Gaia dies. At the same time, Gaia is only middle-aged.

Several times, there have been great dyings. In these a

majority of species then living perished. Each time this has happened, Gaia has slowly nurtured life back, producing a new, diverse set of species through millions of years of patient evolution. Using the species that are left, as our mammalian ancestors were left when the dinosaurs died off, Gaia diversifies species, weaving multiple pathways for the light to move through. Multiple pathways make a more stable pattern for the tapestry of life as a whole; were there only a few, the loss of any would rend the pattern. As Gaia's weaving through time evolves more diverse species, the loss of any will mean less in the overall design. And Gaia always has an eye on the whole tapestry. Hence Gaia's aesthetic preference for diversity.

Where do we fit into Gaia's tapestry of life? Are we special because we are self-conscious? There is no reason to think so. Gaia is not self-conscious in the way we are. Gaia might not recognize us as self-conscious, any more than we think bacteria self-conscious. For Gaia, we are, like all species, a pathway for energy that Gaia uses as it regulates global conditions. All species are this to Gaia: pathways through which energy and light can move to produce stable conditions through time. Gaia is both nurturing and impersonal. Gaian love is tough love.

The popular notion that we have a special place within Gaia because we are self-conscious repeats Ptolemy's error. Ptolemy believed the Earth the center of the Universe. We believed it along with him for thirteen hundred years, until Copernicus taught us that the Earth orbits the Sun. We need to effect a Copernican shift in our view of ourselves as a species that places us within the greater life of Gaia. We will remain alive as human beings as long as we fit into the Gaian tapestry. If we do not, our place in the design will be erased by Gaia for the sake of the overall design. One has to admire the breadth of the Gaian view and the justice of it.

Emerging Global Wisdom

Which brings us to the global impact of our actions. Only in the last few decades have we had a global impact on Gaian systems. Now we change the global temperature, the ozone layer, the percentage of land mass covered by forest, and we control a preponderance of the Earth's productive capacity.

What about our consciousness in relation to these global changes? How can we gain a global wisdom equal in scope to our actions?

Recall that Gaia works continuously to keep conditions right for life. It uses rain forests to cool the tropics, ocean algae to produce clouds over the oceans, and so reflect some of the Sun's energy away into space; it uses all living and non-living systems to maintain global conditions; it uses its whole body and mind.

Because we are now modifying some of the main systems Gaia keeps in balance, Gaia will have to respond. We are entering into a direct relationship with Gaia for the first time, a call and response that we have precipitated by our actions. We do not know how Gaia will respond: with a hotter global climate; with a subsequent ice age; we have no idea.

What if Gaia presses on us directly? Our bodies and minds are constituent parts of Gaia, after all, and all of Gaia is what Gaia uses. Suppose Gaia pressures us in such a way as to cause rapid evolution in human consciousness. This would perhaps be the simplest way for Gaia to achieve the stability and balance it needs to restore as a result of our global actions.

From the Gaian perspective, evolution may be no mysterious thing. Although we generally explain it as natural selection working with random variations through time in response to local conditions, it may look quite different to Gaia.

Imagine evolution from inside the mind of Gaia.

Let yourself enter again into the mind of Gaia, and see the tapestry of light that is life: the billions of organisms are threads and the millions of species are designs in the weave. Imagine that as the tapestry evolves through time, Gaia exerts a pull on the design.

When Gaia sees a place in the tapestry that could be enriched by design, it "thinks" that a species should evolve to fill that space. Imagine Gaia's thought acting like the gravity well we met in the Eureka Practice, or like a basin of attraction in chaos theory. Gaia's thought pulls random changes into coherent patterns over a much shorter span of time than were natural selection to operate on its own.

Imagine this: Gaia sees that a way to bring our newly global human action into harmony with the overall pattern is to help our consciousness evolve until we can appreciate our place in the overall pattern and so harmonize with it. Because this is the most parsimonious strategy, Gaia uses it first. If it works, Gaia moves to other business. If it fails, Gaia raises global temperature dramatically, or whatever is the next best option.

If Gaia were to put pressure on our consciousness to evolve, what would it feel like? Can we describe it in a way that fits the patterns of our practice and helps us see into the birth of wisdom? We can indeed, and the coherence of the story is a comfort in our troubled times, when chaos seems ascendant.

To see how Gaia may help us to a global wisdom, recall how wisdom emerges in the individual mind. When we accumulate a certain amount of understanding, wisdom emerges spontaneously. Wisdom is a simplifying pattern on a higher level of organization, an algorithm for action.

We can imagine the birth of wisdom in the consensus mind, the mind we share. The consensus mind as we know it now conspicuously lacks wisdom. If this mind gained wisdom, human consciousness would move across a great divide. How could this happen?

Let us see it together in our minds:

Imagine a million people gathered together in a vast square. Imagine the consensus mind as a grayish, reddish, smoggy cloud of light hanging just around the level of the ears of everyone in the crowd.

Now imagine that a few people start entering the crowd who have experienced the birth of wisdom in their own consciousness in a profound way. These people look different. There is a white light above their heads.

Imagine now that two, three, a hundred of these people enter the crowd, bringing this white light with them. So far each is just an individual, just a solitary beacon in the smog. But let them keep entering.

When a thousand have entered, or perhaps two or three thousand, something begins to happen spontaneously. Just as wisdom emerges spontaneously in the individual mind. Just as Gaia emerged spontaneously when life first covered Earth.

All of a sudden, the scene shifts radically: a geometric projection of white light emerges at a higher level than the lights of the awakened individuals. It dissipates some of the smog of gray and red. It softly illuminates the entire million.

People feel the change to different degrees, but they all feel it. The mood in the crowd shifts, becomes safer and more open.

What we have just seen is the birth of a consensus wisdom, a new global wisdom. It emerges spontaneously when enough individuals gain access to wisdom, precisely as wisdom emerges in the individual when enough understanding accumulates. In both of these cases, a quantitative increase leads, at a certain critical threshold, to a qualitative change.

Superordinate wisdom emerges like a superorganism does: Gaia when life first covered the globe; an ant colony when a young queen has enough of her newly hatched daughters around her. It is an emergent property of the wisdom of individuals.

Why has superordinate wisdom never emerged before? Perhaps because wisdom was rare in the past; perhaps because it did not need to emerge while our global impacts were limited.

Can it emerge now? Only if enough of us are willing to walk into the forests of our hearts and meet and release our beasts. Only then will the cells be born that can support the birth of the new wisdom's body. When we see practice in this way, we begin to see that our own awakening is not just for ourselves but for the sake of everyone and everything.

Emerging Global Mind

Global wisdom has yet to emerge. Our actions, however, are already global. The hardware and software of our mind are now going global, though we do not yet know what end they will serve. Only wisdom remains to go global; the need for it to do so is achingly obvious.

Before looking further into global wisdom, though, we need to look into how our mind is going global. The place to start is here: as a species, we have already merged with our machines. This is a thrilling thing to have done. Our bodies and senses now have a superhuman reach, and our mind is not far behind. Airplanes and cars extend the reach of our bodies; telecommunications extend the reach of our persona; spacecraft let us visit other planets through their delicate sensors; computers extend the range of our memory and thought; television cameras extend the range of our eyes and microphones the range of our ears. The Internet is rapidly letting individual human minds link together in novel patterns of planetwide relationship. The only life we now know how to lead depends intimately on our instrumentalities. Like all great changes, it happened before we knew it. Nothing we thought about it beforehand had much to do with the reality of the change.

There have long been science fiction fantasies that we would one day become cyborgs. In this grim picture, future human beings become half-machine, with wires and gears replacing our arms, computers patched directly into our brains, our humanity lost to the dictates of a mechanical reality. These were crude imaginings. What happened is far subtler. We did not need to graft metal to bone, wire to neuron. Instead we followed the path laid down in our cells: we became symbionts with our machines.

On a social level, we raise and distribute food, make political and business decisions, and give our bodies to the care of doctors, all in ways that depend thoroughly on the electronic and mechanical extensions of ourselves. As a species we have already merged with our machines. It is not something we need to debate or imagine. We live in a new permanent symbiosis with them.

Imagine your life without television, video, phones, answering machines, faxes, computers, E-mail, cars, airplanes; without refrigeration, mechanized farms, medicine. Imagine turning off the national power grid. The greenest of us are just as symbiotic with our instrumentalities as all the rest of us. Even tribesmen from the Amazon now use planes to move their bodies around the planet so they can raise funds to save their homelands.

Let us turn now to the global flow of information, the hardware and software of our mind going global. The Internet has an important role analogous to the central nervous system. Though the Internet is young, crude, and slow, it will evolve rapidly. It is easy to foresee it, and pathways like it, carrying millions of times the information it now does. Already there is a powerful global information flow on the Net. Television and phone and fax are parallel conduits. This flow of information has already substantially changed how we behave as a species. We can see how the world financial markets have become a single market as a result of this flow. Manufacturing is rapidly becoming globally dispersed as the flow and transportation evolve. The Tienanmen Square uprising depended on fax. For many people under thirty, the closest human community is already on the Net.

Information flow is one of the field marks of mind. As the stream of information increases, there is a threshold at which mind emerges. Mind is an emergent property of the flow of information when the flow is coherent and plentiful enough. It may be difficult to define the threshold at which mind appears. But we can see it in ourselves; we can see it in a wide range of living creatures; we can see it in Gaia.

Mind is in the process of going global. Because of the quantity of information we move around the globe, we already think and act differently. Symbiotic with our instrumentalities, our mind now has the same global reach as our actions. As time goes on, the flow of information will increase exponentially, and the global quality of our mind will become ever more apparent. Global mind will soon be as self-evident as our own mind is to us.

There is a dark side to all this. What is to prevent our mind gone global from being as captive to and moved by greed and ignorance as our consensus mind is now? What is to prevent it from using its increasing power in service of narrow views? We need to turn now to the consensus mind, and see how it can evolve.

Homo Gaians

We are poised on a cusp of history. We have the potential to become a new species. One so different in our powers and perspective from the beings we now are that our descendants will merit a new name: *Homo gaians*.

There are three preconditions to the emergence of this new human. First, our action must be global in scale. This has already happened. Second, our mind must become global, both in its infrastructure and in the flow of information. This is happening now. Third, we need to gain access to global wisdom. This has not happened; this is the work we need to do.

How could *Homo gaians* emerge?

To see how, we have to look into an exciting and new area of evolutionary theory. Although the standard model of evolution posits that new species emerge through selection working on variation, that is not, we now know, the only way it happens.

Remarkably, that is not the way the cells in our bodies evolved. The work of the biologist Lynn Margulis, now generally accepted, elucidates how these cells evolved. Let us look into her notion and then see how it applies to continued human evolution.

When life emerged almost four billion years ago, it was

bacterial life, which flourished for a billion and a half years or so before the next great leap happened. During their long reign, bacteria diversified widely. They spent much of their time exchanging genetic material and eating each other. It is crucial to our story that although bacteria have DNA, their simple internal structure lacks a nucleus. In all organisms more complex than bacteria, each cell has a nucleus, which contains the hereditary DNA. How did cells with a nucleus—every one of our cells—evolve from bacteria that have no nucleus?

By symbiosis, says Margulis. One bacteria tried to eat another and found that the second bacterial cell remained intact inside it. A relationship ensued that was beneficial to both. Over time, they shared tasks—and the modern nucleated cell was born. In this symbiosis, which may have happened many times, cells made an evolutionary leap that would have been completely unpredictable from looking at the cells then existing.

This was evolution by merger. The symbiosis of two entities of similar scale produced an entity unlike any seen before. It was this symbiotic merger that opened the floodgates of evolution, producing every plant and animal that has ever lived on Earth. A powerful symbiosis indeed.

Let us apply this notion of symbiosis now to our own continued evolution.

Begin by seeing that human actions have become global:

See the planetwide impacts we have on weather, ozone, forests. Now let yourself see that the human mind has gone global: see streams of information coursing around the globe, just as blood courses through our arteries.

Now see a step beyond. Imagine that wisdom is about to go global: see patterns of white light, simple, geometric, pleasing, overlaying the whole Earth. Seeing all of these, you are seeing the mind, heart, and action of the global human.

Let yourself feel this human, now global in scope, ready to make the next great evolutionary leap. The leap will be a leap into Gaia, a merger and symbiosis. It will happen spontaneously once our mind, heart, and action go global.

Let us turn our awareness now to our symbiotic partner:

See once again the view of Gaia from space: the great blue living globe. Let yourself feel Gaia alive and covering the globe. Let yourself experience Gaia and the global human, each of them, as planetwide entities, spanning the globe. One is ancient, ineluctable, and tough; the other newborn, fragile.

Now let yourself see us merging, just as the original bacteria merged to form the nucleated cell more than two billion years ago.

Human being merging into Gaia. See the global human mind, heart, and action, with its patterns, combine with the tapestry of light in the mind of Gaia. From two sets of global pattern one emerges, novel, rich, tightly interwoven, inseparable.

Let yourself see the global human and Gaia entering fully into symbiosis, becoming a single global entity. Merging into one organic being, like those two early cells. We become a single entity with billions of individual members. Each with its own vivid life.

All of us conscious, knowing our interdependence with all that lives, feeling it in every atom of our bodies and minds. Our will merged with the will of Gaia. Our thoughts merged with the mind of Gaia. Our heart merged with the love of Gaia.

Our actions selfish on behalf of all beings: Homo gaians.

We can see this new human being at the edge of our vision, but there is no guarantee that he and she will emerge into time. There is no predetermined future; no Omega Point lies unfailingly before us. The future is ours to choose, and we choose it by our practice. If we cannot open to wisdom, catastrophe is certain: Gaia will make adjustments. Life will flourish; we may not.

We now act toward the Earth as hungry biomass with a deadly powerful brain, quickly consuming the fabric of the Gaian tapestry of life. Let us seek wisdom as the way out. If we do, Gaia will ease the way.

It is a revolution in consciousness that we need so we may learn to be fully human upon the Earth. This is the ultimate revolution. And it can only happen at the grass roots. No hierarchies are needed, no new religions, no new dogmas. Each of us, with the support of those we love, must claim the power to open to the wisdom within our own mind and heart and to that encoded in Nature. If each one of us does this, then global wisdom will take care of itself. Once our consensus mind knows harmony, policy will easily follow.

So let us practice toward wisdom: let us take responsibility for every one of our thoughts, feelings, and actions. Let us choose in every moment to be fully present. Let us meet and release all the beasts in the forests of our hearts. Let us choose to evolve.

This is the path of wisdom. Let us walk it with absolute sincerity. Our souls will come forward and our lives will be rich in wonder. Of this there is no doubt. Let us trust in wisdom's Way wherever it takes us, for the sake of all that lives and for everything that ever will.

Now a final task, and a pleasant one it is. It is time to take an afternoon, as you did at the beginning of our journey.

Return to the nihilistic myth of our culture and again turn it into a positive story, line by line.

Take an afternoon when you have time to be alone and let your story emerge. It may be quite a different story this time. Enjoy your storytelling. Treat yourself well: go for a walk in the country; take a long hot bath; eat delicious food; drink your favorite wine. Let your story bubble up, your own myth that makes sense of our life. Then let it flow forth from you in a thousand different ways to bless and enrich those you meet along the Way.

May your journey go well, all your life long!

9

The Song
of the Earth

I have always been singing to you.
It is a love song that I sing you, a song of love and longing.
My song beats within the beat of your mother's heart.
You hear it like a whale song, as you swim in the sea of the
    womb, a salty inlet of my ocean that bore your ancestors.
I whisper it to you through the womb's walls you tear open while
    being born.

I sing it to encourage your first steps as you challenge gravity,
    and when you discover ants.
My song resounds in awe as you enter the awareness of a child,
    brain and consciousness expanding.
I shout it in joyous thunderstorms, and in your very blood, hot
    from your lover's kiss.
When you are betrayed, when you are sick, when you are
    lonely, I still sing to you, my song still fills your lungs and
    beats your heart.

When you are in pain, you must listen closely for my song.
Accept it then, and let it flow through you.
When you do you feel the life it gives you, and begin to sing my
    song yourself.

You sing it quietly, in solitude at first, as if it were a secret you
     can't yet share.
And so you hum it to yourself, and sing it in the bath.
As you open to my song, and let it flow through you, it brings
     happiness, and happiness does not hide.

As your happiness, my song comes forth and shares itself with
     those you meet, and reminds them of the song playing deep
     within themselves.
The song they may have forgotten, but which has never forgotten
     them, for I can never forget a single one of you.
I sing you through the whole of life, and at your death sing
     threnody, a sweet welcome back, and a birth to new
     beginning.

About the Author

A former senior attorney at the Natural Resources Defense Council and editor-in-chief of the *New York University Law Review*, James Thornton took top honors in philosophy at Yale. He is the executive director of the Heffter Research Institute and founder of Positive Futures. He lives in Santa Fe, New Mexico, and the French Pyrenees.

Visit the author at www.soulcompanion.com for monthly meditation, Q&A, and more.

OTHER BELL TOWER BOOKS

*Books that nourish the soul, illuminate the mind,
and speak directly to the heart*

ROB BAKER
PLANNING MEMORIAL CELEBRATIONS
A Sourcebook
A one-stop handbook for a situation more and more of us
are facing as we grow older.
0-609-80404-9 Softcover

THOMAS BERRY
THE GREAT WORK
Our Way into the Future
The grandfather of Deep Ecology teaches us how to move from a
human-centered view of the world to one focused on the earth and all
its inhabitants.
0-609-60525-9 Hardcover

CYNTHIA BOURGEAULT
LOVE IS STRONGER THAN DEATH
The Mystical Union of Two Souls
Both the story of the incandescent love between two hermits
and a guidebook for those called to this path of soulwork.
0-609-60473-2 Hardcover

MADELINE BRUSER
THE ART OF PRACTICING
Making Music from the Heart
A classic work on how to practice music which combines meditative
principles with information on body mechanics and medicine.
0-517-70822-1 Hardcover
0-609-80177-5 Softcover

MELODY ERMACHILD CHAVIS
ALTARS IN THE STREET
A Courageous Memoir of Community and Spiritual Awakening
A deeply moving account that captures
the essence of human struggles and resourcefulness.
0-609-80196-1 Softcover

DAVID A. COOPER
ENTERING THE SACRED MOUNTAIN
Exploring the Mystical Practices of Judaism, Buddhism, and Sufism
An inspiring chronicle of one man's search for truth.
0-517-88464-X Softcover

MARC DAVID
NOURISHING WISDOM
A Mind/Body Approach to Nutrition and Well-Being
A book that advocates awareness in eating.
0-517-88129-2 Softcover

KAT DUFF
THE ALCHEMY OF ILLNESS
A luminous inquiry into the function and purpose of illness.
0-517-88097-0 Softcover

JOAN FURMAN, MSN, RN, AND DAVID McNABB
THE DYING TIME
Practical Wisdom for the Dying and Their Caregivers
A comprehensive guide, filled with physical, emotional,
and spiritual advice.
0-609-80003-5 Softcover

BERNIE GLASSMAN
BEARING WITNESS
A Zen Master's Lessons in Making Peace
How Glassman started the Zen Peacemaker Order and what
each of us can do to make peace in our hearts and in the world.
0-609-80391-3 Softcover

BERNARD GLASSMAN AND RICK FIELDS
INSTRUCTIONS TO THE COOK
A Zen Master's Lessons in Living a Life That Matters
A distillation of Zen wisdom that can be used equally well as
a manual on business or spiritual practice, cooking or life.
0-517-88829-7 Softcover

BURGHILD NINA HOLZER
A WALK BETWEEN HEAVEN AND EARTH
A Personal Journal on Writing and the Creative Process
How keeping a journal focuses and expands our awareness
of ourselves and everything that touches our lives.
0-517-88096-2 Softcover

GREG JOHANSON AND RON KURTZ
GRACE UNFOLDING
Psychotherapy in the Spirit of the Tao-te ching
The interaction of client and therapist illuminated
through the gentle power and wisdom of Lao Tsu's ancient classic.
0-517-88130-6 Softcover

SELECTED BY MARCIA AND JACK KELLY
ONE HUNDRED GRACES
Mealtime Blessings
A collection of graces from many traditions, inscribed in calligraphy
reminiscent of the manuscripts of medieval Europe.
0-517-58567-7 Hardcover
0-609-80093-0 Softcover

JACK AND MARCIA KELLY
SANCTUARIES
*A Guide to Lodgings in Monasteries, Abbeys, and Retreats
of the United States*
For those in search of renewal and a little peace; described by the *New
York Times* as "the *Michelin Guide* of the retreat set."
0-517-88517-4 Softcover

MARCIA AND JACK KELLY
THE WHOLE HEAVEN CATALOG
*A Resource Guide to Products, Services, Arts, Crafts, and Festivals
of Religious, Spiritual, and Cooperative Communities*
All the things that monks and nuns do to support their habits!
0-609-80120-1 Softcover

BARBARA LACHMAN
THE JOURNAL OF HILDEGARD OF BINGEN
A year in the life of the twelfth-century German saint—
the diary she never had the time to write herself.
0-517-88390-2 Softcover

STEPHEN LEVINE
A YEAR TO LIVE
How to Live This Year as if It Were Your Last
Using the consciousness of our mortality to enter into
a new and vibrant relationship with life.
0-609-80194-5 Softcover

GUNILLA NORRIS
BEING HOME
A Book of Meditations
An exquisite modern book of hours,
a celebration of mindfulness in everyday activities.
0-517-58159-0 Hardcover

MARCIA PRAGER
THE PATH OF BLESSING
Experiencing the Energy and Abundance of the Divine
How to use the traditional Jewish practice of calling down a blessing
on each action as a profound path of spiritual growth.
0-517-70363-7 Hardcover
0-609-80393-X Softcover

SAKI SANTORELLI
HEAL THY SELF
Lessons on Mindfulness in Medicine
An invitation to patients and health-care professionals to bring
mindfulness into the crucible of the healing relationship.
0-609-60385-X Hardcover
0-609-80504-5 Softcover

RABBI RAMI M. SHAPIRO
MINYAN
Ten Principles for Living a Life of Integrity
A primer for those interested to know
what Judaism has to offer the spiritually hungry.
0-609-80055-8 Softcover

RABBI RAMI M. SHAPIRO
WISDOM OF THE JEWISH SAGES
A Modern Reading of Pirke Avot
A third-century treasury of maxims on justice, integrity, and virtue—
Judaism's principal ethical scripture.
0-517-79966-9 Hardcover

JEAN SMITH
THE BEGINNER'S GUIDE TO ZEN BUDDHISM
A comprehensive and easily accessible introduction
that assumes no prior knowledge of Zen Buddhism.
0-609-80466-9 Softcover

Rabbi Joseph Telushkin
THE BOOK OF JEWISH VALUES
A Day-by-Day Guide to Ethical Living
Ancient and modern advice on how to remain honest in a
morally complicated world.
0-609-60330-2 Hardcover

Joan Tollifson
BARE-BONES MEDITATION
Waking Up from the Story of My Life
An unvarnished, exhilarating account of one woman's struggle
to make sense of her life.
0-517-88792-4 Softcover

Michael Toms and Justine Willis Toms
TRUE WORK
Doing What You Love and Loving What You Do
Wisdom for the workplace from the husband-and-wife team
of NPR's weekly radio program *New Dimensions.*
0-517-70587-7 Hardcover
0-609-80212-7 Softcover

Ed. Richard Whelan
SELF-RELIANCE
The Wisdom of Ralph Waldo Emerson as Inspiration for Daily Living
A distillation of Emerson's spiritual writings
for contemporary readers.
0-517-58512-X Softcover

*Bell Tower books are for sale at your local bookstore
or you may call Random House at* 1-800-793-BOOK
to order with a credit card.